TEST
YOUR
CHILD

TEST
YOUR
CHILD

*How to discover and enhance your
child's true potential*

DR. MIRIAM STOPPARD

DORLING KINDERSLEY . LONDON

A
DORLING KINDERSLEY
BOOK

First published
in Great Britain in 1991
by Dorling Kindersley Limited,
9 Henrietta Street, London WC2E 8PS

Conceived, edited and designed by
CARROLL & BROWN LIMITED
12 Colas Mews
London NW6 4LH

Editorial Director Amy Carroll
Art Director Denise Brown
Art Editor Tracy Timson

A CIP catalogue record for this book is available
from the British Library

ISBN 0–86318 600 9

Printed and bound in
Singapore by Toppan

CONTENTS

PARENT AS TEACHER

THE NORMAL COURSE
OF DEVELOPMENT

PREFACE

Test Your Child is a controversial title for this book. The word "test" may be emotive and to some parents, worrying. Yet I have used it deliberately. It is, after all, the word used by paediatricians, health workers, and other members of the medical profession whose daily concern is the health and development of many children.

I have used the word "test" because I believe parents should take more control. "How can I best help my child?" is the question I am asked most often, and only by observing, monitoring, and understanding your child can you judge what he or she is capable of, and help him or her to achieve it. Increasing the potential of one's child is every parent's dearest wish but to do so, you must be confident about your child's abilities. I wrote *Test Your Child* to help parents explore their children's skills and talents, and to explain how to create the home environment that encourages development of these skills, as far as they are in each child to develop.

Throughout the text, I emphasise that you should take the lead from your child, reject any notion of "force-feeding," and strive to keep the pressure off. I was pressured during my childhood and still fear failure; I would like to guarantee that your child avoids any such experience.

Test Your Child should enable you to enjoy your child and get close to him or her in ways you won't have dreamed of; this is what all the activities and exercises are about. And it should help you to see your child as he or she really is. Parents who are unrealistic about what their child can achieve only produce unhappiness. But those who are able to assess their child's abilities, and adjust their expectations and assistance accordingly, will become their child's best resource.

THE PARENT AS TEACHER

As a parent, you are called on to play many roles in your child's life. One of the most important is to create a loving and stimulating environment for your child. Another is to monitor his or her healthy development. Another is to encourage in your child a good self-image, though we know of no single factor that is absolutely essential to help your child develop this. But what we do know is that consistent unconditional acceptance, concern, sympathy and respect, maintaining a sharing, dignified relationship with you, and encouraging freedom and independence with clearly defined limits are certainly the best bases from which to build one.

We now know that a child starts to absorb information from the moment he or she is born, and it is from parents that a child gets most of his or her information. Parents, therefore, become totally responsible for their child's early learning and their role as teachers is great.

SKILLS THAT ENCOURAGE LEARNING

A parent is responsible for encouraging imagination, instilling discipline, and teaching helpfulness, amongst other things. It is important, therefore, for parents to make use of skills that will help them to do their job better.

Set appropriate goals

Beware of setting goals that are ill defined or constantly outstrip your child's abilities. Never pursue perfection as this will lead to frustration both to your child and to you, and you will end up with an unhappy, demoralised child who simply cannot thrive and develop well. Never fall into the trap of expecting too much too soon, but be aware of the small accomplishments and successes that your child achieves every day. Try not to focus on deficiencies; concentrate instead on noticing and praising every single positive act or advance.

Over-indulgence is equally hard on your child. Your motives are, no doubt, good hearted, but pampering and spoiling and

over-protecting your child can keep your child dependent, feeling helpless, and possibly cause him to take up the role of a victim, which will make life very difficult to cope with indeed.

Always join in

One of the jobs of being a teacher to your child is that you actually have to DO THINGS. In fact, you have to do many more things than you may feel like doing. Your child learns through example and imitation until she is over eight years old, and one of the best ways to show her a good example is to get up and do something in front of her, or with her. This means that you do not rely on just giving your child orders or directions. For example, instead of correcting your child by saying "Do not eat with your fingers," pick up your spoon and very purposefully go through the motions yourself while saying "we eat with our spoon." Instead of telling her to, "Go and tidy up your toys," you need to take your child by the hand, get down on your knees, and make a game of doing it together, saying "It is time to put your toys away." Movement combined with the smallest amount of fantasy or good humour, a joke, or a game, goes a long way toward getting your child to do what you want, such as clearing away the toys.

You can join in with your child's games rather than interrupting them, so, if the children are playing train drivers suggest that the train moves into the station instead of in the road while you start tidying up and moving the chairs out of the way. You could ask the truckdriver (your daughter) to steer the truck into its garage or to get the cowboy (your son) to ride the horse into the stable.

Repeat, repeat, repeat

With all children, but especially young children, it is frustrating but necessary to tell them over and over again to do the same thing. For example, a young child will not sit calmly while he is having a snack, eating lunch or waiting for anything. So you may have to repeat certain messages like "We do not swing our legs and kick the chair while we are eating" for months and months and months until your child's body gets the message as well as his mind.

Give positive examples

Remember, whenever possible, to state something in a positive way. Say "Yes that is a nice little dog; let's pat the dog" and

you show your child how to do it. Then take her hand and demonstrate the movement with her. Do not shriek "Don't hurt the little puppy." Sentences that begin with "do not," communicate displeasure from the moment you start to speak. An infant's brain, however, does not necessarily process every word, so in the case above, your message may come out as ". . . hurt . . . puppy!" – your opposite intention.

It is not until school age that a child is ready to respond to instructions expressed only through words unaccompanied by actions. So, whenever you can, act out your words and give your child a picture of the actions. Make them dramatic, theatrical, and overdone. Instead of saying, "Do not slam the door when you come in!", go to the door when you hear your son, welcome him there and then say "We close the door quietly" while you move his hand very gently through the motion of closing the door; then repeat the motion with the door knob in his hand closing the door quietly.

Make sure your child can remember instructions

You cannot expect your child to remember correct behaviour, even though you have demonstrated it again and again, until your child's memory is mature. Learning is acquired through gradual maturation and the repetition of actions, which enable habits to form in your child.

You should not expect your child to begin to remember what she should and should not do before the age of five. Once her memory is mature enough things are remembered after only a few tellings and much more quickly.

Don't interrupt

A lot of children have difficulty with concentration span and it is difficult to foster because a small child simply cannot concentrate as well as an adult. One of the major things you can do to help your child sustain attention is not to interrupt when he is clearly absorbed in something. Save your intervention until his attention has moved on to something else, but then praise him for a job well done.

Give attention

For a very young child giving attention has to be dramatic and obvious. A child is very sensitive to whether you are taking notice or not, and will either pull you up for not giving your full attention, or take hold of your hand or clothes in order to attract

your attention. A child only feels that she is being listened to if you make eye contact and stop what you are doing in order to listen, and this you must do. If you do this from a very early age, your child will know that she has a voice, and that you respect her as an individual.

Know when to forbid

Even though you may show your child by example and state things positively, there have to be times when you need to say "no" to your child, and your child must understand that when you say "no" whatever he is doing is forbidden. After a great deal of thinking, however, I found only three situations where it was absolutely necessary to say no to a child. In our house these were:
□ When my child was going to do anything harmful to himself; for instance, reaching for a cooking pot on the stove, especially one filled with a hot liquid.
□ When my child's actions could have been harmful to others, for example, something as simple as playing noisily or banging his toys about a sleeping baby.
□ When my child's action would result in real damage; for example, when he wanted to use his crayons on the sitting room wall. Even when you say "no" it does not have to

be done in the form of a head-on confrontation and a battle of wills. The best possible way to do it is to distract your child with something else that you know she is very interested in. As far as the coat and sweater example is concerned, you simply go and get it and put it on your child, the alternative being her not playing outside.

It is always worth pausing for a moment before you decide to say no to make sure you know exactly what your child intends, and that your answer is the correct one. Keeping discipline simple and consistent is important so that your child knows what you mean, knows you mean what you say, and that your word is followed immediately by an expected action.

In terms of disciplining a child it is impossible to make her do the right thing, because she does not have the intellectual power to distinguish between right and wrong; also her will is very strong. You must understand that your baby does not do things in relation to you, and cannot change her behaviour, because you want her to, so there is no point in insisting on it.

Up to the age of three your baby's will changes from an instinct to an urge, then to a desire, and finally, to a motive. Around the age of two and a half, an emotional

element enters. At this age, however, it doesn't help to say why you want children to do things, because they have not yet awakened to the idea of having a motive for doing something. Your three year old is incapable of acting with reflection, and if you ask her to try to understand her own motives she will be incapable; reasoning comes very much later — in some children, as late as adolescence.

REARING HELPFUL CHILDREN

Children of a very young age, even less than two years old, show helpful, generous, and kind behaviour especially towards mum, but towards others as well. It is also true that some children show more kindness and altruism than others. Most of us would like our children to behave in this helpful way so here are a few tips as to how you can create a family environment that seems to foster this kind of child.

Create a loving family climate
Parents who believe in loving, nurturing, and supporting their children have children who are more helpful, more empathetic, and more thoughtful towards others. This probably reflects the secure attachment of the child to the parent and the effect of your good moods. Undoubtedly it also reflects the fact that the child models her behaviour on your behaviour. Your child is much more likely to help someone if she is in a good mood so it is worth trying to keep her that way.

Give rules and explain why
One of the reasons why a completely undisciplined upbringing is bad for children is that they thrive better and develop better with a slightly authoritative parental style.

By and large, children like to have clear guidelines about rules and standards. It is a pattern that fosters high self-esteem and popularity.

Parents who both explain the consequence of a child's action "If you hit Jimmy it will hurt him" and who, in addition, state the rules clearly, explicitly, and with emotion "You mustn't hit people!" rear children who are more likely to react to others with sympathy and helpfulness. There is much research showing that stating the reason for generosity or helpfulness, particularly if the reason focuses on the feelings of others, helps a child to behave in a kind, thoughtful way.

All parents spend a lot of time telling children what not to do, and it is very important to tell children why they should not do things — especially in terms of the effect it will have on others. It is also important to have positive rules which you should repeat ad nauseam, for example "It is always good to be helpful to other people who are less fortunate."

Set useful tasks
Letting children do really helpful things around the house or in school such as cooking, taking care of pets, making toys to give to unfortunate children, or teaching younger brothers and sisters how to play games, fosters helpfulness in most children. Of course, not all children do such things spontaneously and have to be asked, encouraged, and sometimes even coerced, though coercion must be gentle otherwise it has the opposite effect.

The most significant way to rear helpful children is to demonstrate to your children the generous, thoughtful, and helpful behaviour you would like them to show. When there is a conflict between what you say and what you do, children will imitate what you do, so it is simply not good enough to state the rules or guidelines clearly if your behaviour does not echo what you say.

USING DISCIPLINE POSITIVELY

Discipline is more than correcting undesirable behaviour. It also means helping your child to develop in a healthy way, mentally, emotionally, and physically. With a baby we look after her physical body, then we lead our toddler by giving her day punctuation and rhythm, and then, as she becomes older, we literally take her by the hand and try to be an example ourselves. Only at school age is your child aided by stories and the spoken word, without example from you.

It is not really appropriate to correct bad behaviour and expect your child to repeat what you think is the right action. What you should remember is that actions need to be corrected at the present moment without any hope of your child remembering the next time, and this will help you to keep your temper, and model the right behaviour over and over again. What you are aiming for is firmness, imbued with love. Most children respond to some discipline and a lot of rhythm in home life. By rhythm I mean morning routines and night-time routines — snack time, lunch time, play time, nap time, bath time. Children thrive on pattern and a regular life style. A rhythm to life very quickly becomes a habit, and an extremely enjoyable one. Your home's rhythms become accepted as the norm, and this will help to eliminate many difficulties, struggles, and arguments about eating, bathing, and going to bed. Most experts who work with children state that they need some form of structure in

their outside world to continue to grow healthily and enjoy emotional well being. It is also an environment that encourages learning — it allows a time for all things. You can encourage this concept with the commentary "Now is the time for you to play," "Now you can do anything you like," "Now is the time for a meal," "Now is the time for a nap," "Now is the time for a bath," etc. You can use any of these punctuations in your child's daily life as an opportunity for teaching your child.

Meal times
Eating together is a major activity of most families, and it is one of the best ways of bringing your family together and teaching your child how to interact with a group. You have to be careful, however, that meal times never turn into battle-grounds or become chaotic, and that a certain degree of ritual is observed so that family members do not just arrive at the table, grab something and eat on the run.

The important thing is to have meals at regular times because it is helpful for creating a rhythm in family life. As my children got older and went to different schools and my husband and I had different working times, we still felt "held close" by breakfast. This was the time when we started the day together, and to do so, we all had to get up in time to eat with the child who departed earliest. Not a day went by when we did not have breakfast all together and it gave us a feeling of great strength and security to do so.

I believe that certain behaviour should be insisted on at meal times so there can be a calm and harmonious experience for all the family. Small children especially need to eat in quiet, calm surroundings without interruptions from the radio, television, or somebody banging about playing.

If your child becomes whiny or throws a tantrum, take him out immediately, not to his bedroom, which he will learn to hate, but into a room where there are plenty of toys available for distraction. However, you will find that if you do this the first time your child throws a fit, he will probably change his behaviour and come back in a few minutes because he simply does not want to miss the action.

Do not try to conduct adult conversations at meal times, because children need to be accepted as participants in meal-time conversations. You have to pick your subject matter and the way you express things, so that meal times are not only a time of eating, but also of listening, sharing, balancing conversation, making contributions, and learning to fit in with others.

Many things we do in life have a formal ending, so give meal times this kind of wrap-up. Children should not be allowed to get down without saying that they have finished and asking to be excused, but, of course, they cannot be expected to do this until they are over the age of four or possibly five. Having your child ask to be excused at the end of a meal is not simply old fashioned, it is a useful way to keep track of who has finished eating.

Going to bed and waking up times

Bed time does not have to be a particular time rigidly adhered to, but it should have some kind of regular proceedings, a kind of ritual, which the child remembers and looks forward to as a happy wind down to the day. She should know as soon as the first ritual is set in motion that there is an hour or so of lovely times with mum and dad to look forward to. This in itself induces quietness, calmness, tranquility, and even sleepiness in your child as you gradually work toward sitting on the edge of the bed with her telling a bedtime story, or singing a song and then curling up on the bed so that she goes to sleep in the security of your arms. If you make bed times pleasant, and devote some time and thought to them and try, for instance, to stop your child being upset so that sleep becomes difficult, your child will naturally grow into a phase around the age of six when she gravitates to bed of her own accord, without any prompting from you, as soon as she feels tired and without making a fuss or procrastinating.

I have always believed that how a child goes to sleep is important for refreshing her mind and spirit as well as her body. I have always felt a great desire that my child

should go to sleep without being upset, and certainly without crying. I therefore let small misdemeanours near bedtime pass by without as much as a reference, so that my child will be tranquil when it is time to go to sleep. I have always been of the conviction that the misdemeanour can be corrected, if repeated, at another time, when my child is feeling stronger, and does not need sleep so much.

With your young child almost the whole time after dinner is directed toward bed time. You can quieten down play by straightening up the room, then a bath or washing, brushing the teeth, and putting on pyjamas, when there can be gentle games and lots of interplay between you and your child. At this time of day talking slowly, or singing softly can help procure a quiet sleep-inducing mood for bedtime. If you make sure that the lighting is gentle, using a nightlight for instance, and then whisper for ten to twenty minutes with your child who is ready for bed, you help create a mood of calmness, love, and sharing.

Just as going to sleep in a good frame of mind is important so is waking up cheerfully. Mornings should be happy times so it is worth putting some time and effort into preparing for them. For instance, if you lay your child's clothes out with him, he will start dressing himself at an earlier age than he might have done otherwise. It is also possible to get ready sports gear, exercise books, lunches, etc., the night before so that you can concentrate simply on making mornings a happy time.

In most families, the biggest problem with mornings is being rushed, and this has the effect of making children move more and more slowly, which can put the whole family in a bad mood. If you have more time you will not give your child a shock awakening because children do need time to make the transition from sleep to consciousness as gently as possible — just as we do. Your child may retain a kind of night-consciousness after wakening, so for ten to fifteen minutes she is unable to cope with any kind of questions or rapid activity or remember to do things like brushing her teeth. So try to avoid questions and asking your child to make choices. Also, you should try to bring a particular order to the way in which your child goes about her morning routine, like first getting out of bed, then going to the bathroom, followed by brushing her teeth, washing her face, and combing her hair, then getting dressed, coming downstairs, and having breakfast.

Daily tasks

It is a good idea from infancy to give your child a small task to do every day. In doing so you are laying down good habits for a lifetime in terms of responsibility, punctuality, and having respect for people and things. So you might ask your child to do something simple like watering a plant, feeding the rabbits, feeding the fish, or reading the barometer, etc.

As your child gets older you can give him activities that occur on the same day of each week. So, you might go for a walk in the park on Monday, to the swimming pool on Tuesday, to the shops on Wednesday, to play with friends on Thursday, or have special home activities like painting, water games, or playing in the sand pit on Friday. Then, of course, there are the rhythms of the year and the celebrations that punctuate twelve months. Birthdays are the most obvious ones, Christmas is another, Easter might be another, summer holiday would be another, but, in fact, you can commemorate anything you like. You might make a point of celebrating the beginning of each season, which gives all kinds of scope for activities, like drawing what the world looks like. You could point out the trees with and without leaves, the changing colours of the season, the changing weather, different activities, playing with snowmen in winter and going to the seaside and swimming in the summer.

All our family found the punctuation of the seasons thrilling, exciting, and a source of great security. It also helped our children to learn about nature, the way the world works, the way animals live, and to become environmentally and ecologically aware.

COMMUNICATING SUCCESSFULLY WITH YOUR CHILD

I think children should always be allowed to talk, and not only about acceptable and undangerous subjects, but to raise controversy and debate. To my mind, this is an essential ingredient in the development of a good self-image, in self-assurance, and in a feeling that what a child does and says matters, and therefore, a feel for what is a child's right and the limit of what is socially allowable in terms of social discourse.

I was determined that my children would feel free to bring any subject, no matter how taboo, into the home and discuss it with supportive parents rather than being furtive and looking for help elsewhere. When my four-year-old son first

asked me if I wanted to hear a dirty joke I had a moment's hesitation and realized that it was crunch time. I smiled and said brightly that I would love to hear his dirty joke, which turned out to be childishly lavatorial. However, I felt that it broke the ice and established a pattern of my children being able to raise any subject in the house without being criticised and turned away.

As your child grows older she will question your decisions, challenge your logic, be unafraid about presenting an opposing point of view, and enter into true adult debate without losing her temper. It is very important that your child learns to do all of these things in the security and safety of a loving home, before taking her exchanges into the public arena.

Before any teacher does it, you have to show that the ability to think for oneself is valued. Do not, therefore, reward right answers and punish wrong ones. Good parents do not rush to point out or correct all their child's mistakes as soon as they are made. If you do this your child's own self-checking and self-correcting skills will not develop sufficiently; he also will gain very little self confidence.

Adults enjoy the rules of polite disagreement and these should apply equally to any parent – child interaction. Using them you will help your child to form opinions, strengthen his logic, and teach him how to question things in a genuine and confident way. You can allow your son to state his case and disagree with your views, in a friendly atmosphere. A good parent feels proud of his or her child's growing mental ability and confidence, and is not threatened by disagreements.

Developing a "what if" attitude in your child is a good thing to help anticipate, so that she is able to consider several different alternatives at the same time. So, when your child impulsively suggests an inappropriate action, just stop her and ask her to consider what will happen if she goes ahead and does that, and let her arrive on her own at the reasons why it is an unsuitable action. This way she will learn to think out the consequence of her actions when she does not have you or anybody else around to help.

All of these things encourage your child to think further ahead, and therefore, encourage the delay of self gratification for a longer and longer period, which helps judgement and social maturity. It is the ability to inhibit spontaneous desires that signals emotional growth.

THE NORMAL COURSE OF DEVELOP-MENT

UNDERSTANDING THE STAGES OF DEVELOPMENT

As your child develops, her progress is inexorable and the pace at which she will develop is singular to her, but it can be encouraged and spurred on by you. What cannot be changed by you is the sequence through which her developmental changes will pass.

SOME GENERALISATIONS

Development is continuous. In certain areas it may slow down but it never ceases and at times, development in certain areas will proceed at what seems to be the cost of all others. In terms of the speed of development, no two children are the same. So, for instance, your child has to sit before he can walk, but the exact times at which he begins to sit and walk will be different from all other children.

Development also is completely dependent on how mature the brain, nervous system, and other body parts have become; a child cannot walk until her nervous system, muscles and joints have reached sufficient maturity. Similarly, and most importantly, no child can be dry at night or have control over her bowels until all the nervous connections have been made between the brain, spinal cord, bladder and bowel, and no amount of potty sitting can change that.

Speech is dependent on muscle and brain development; until the mouth enlarges, the palate becomes arched, and the tongue smaller,(between 24 to 36 weeks), the waves and muscles of speech cannot produce the sounds needed for words. Sufficient brain development to "speak" is not usual before the age of 12 months. Only after this stage of development is reached can speech be "taught". Some babies say their first word as early as 32 weeks, others as late as three or four years. Girls, as a rule, speak earlier than boys. Nouns, names of things, make up your child's first words. Verbs come afterwards.

By observing your child closely you will notice that development always proceeds from head to foot, no matter what the skill that is being mastered. So, strange though it may seem, the first stage of walking is control of the head; maintaining balance and stepping on two feet is the very last.

As your child gets older you will notice that skills become finer and more refined as your baby matures. So the first attempts at speech are seen in jogging and bobbing movements of the whole body, even waving of the hands and arms and kicking of the legs until finally speech is confined to movements of the mouth and facial expressions.

CHARTING DEVELOPMENT

In order to provide parents with a "road map" of how their child will develop the special skills such as walking, talking, socialising, bowel and bladder control, I have created a series of illustrated charts.

Remember, only one aspect of the charts applies to every child and that is the sequence of developmental changes that is followed as the skill is fully acquired. The speed and ease of acquisition is individual to each child, and therefore all the times and ages given should be interpreted as rough guides only. In fact, doctors tend to use average figures and, in reality, the average does not exist since it is arrived at arithmetically, not by observation. So the chances of your child doing anything exactly at a stated time are very low; your child will do it earlier or later.

WORKING WITH YOUR CHILD

To give the right help at the right time in order to maximise the chances of your child reaching his or her full potential you must match your efforts to your child's stage of development. Therefore, an important element in the charts is constructive suggestions about your role as helper and educator. The suggestions are simple, practical and in most instances, effortless. In fact, they are the kind of things that good parents do without ever thinking. What they do assume is a happy, outgoing child, confident in parental love. Nowhere have I indicated where, when, how often or for how long you should engage in these activities because they should be spontaneous and they have a natural length. In general, any opportunity for games, play and closeness is a good time, and your baby's boredom indicates when you should stop. So I would say about four or five times a day for three or four minutes each time as a minimum.

The activities are not there so you can make your child especially bright. Rather, they subserve the hope that you will not form unrealistic goals for your child, that you will not push, force, or pressure your child to reach arbitrary standards but work alongside him or her in a purely supportive way. As children learn more in the first years of life than at any other time, parents have enormous responsibilities to be caring, patient teachers to pre-school children.

To me, the idea of parent as teacher is irresistible; it is a role that should be fun and infinitely rewarding also.

Before you begin to study the charts, you will find it interesting to read the general information that relates to the acquisition of the individual skills. Here, you will find out how best to relate to your child's changing ways, and a few pointers on how to provide a safe and happy environment in which he or she can thrive.

MENTAL DEVELOPMENT

During the first year a baby's brain doubles in weight. The gain in weight is due partly to an increase in the number of brain cells and partly to the growth of "connections" between cells and different parts of the brain. Without these connections we cannot think, and it is through these connections that learning begins. The connections in a newborn baby start to form a network when the baby becomes interested in something and makes a mental effort. This your baby does when any of her senses are stimulated. So from the moment of birth, sounds, sights, touches, feelings, smells, and tastes make more connections.

Developing general understanding involves many parts coming together. Sight, sound, memory, and motor skills must move forward together for mental growth to proceed. The intellect is dependent on the senses and body movement for the baby to understand what is going on around her. For instance, without sight, a baby can't see a toy; without memory, a baby won't get excited by her favourite toy; without brain/muscle coordination, a baby can't reach out to the moving toy; without hand/eye coordination, a baby can't grasp the toy; without holding and playing with the toy, a baby can't form a concept of what that toy is.

Many brain and body skills advance on a tide of growth and expansion as general understanding increases. The determining factors are your baby's sociability and personality, and the environment you create for him.

You can help your child's brain to grow and develop by providing the stimulation as set out in the chart, and it is particularly important for you to do so in the first year of life, and again in the third year, both times when the brain goes through major growth spurts.

NEWBORN

Your baby starts to "understand" at birth. Day 1 she listens and is alert; day 3 she responds when spoken to and her gaze is intent; day 9 her eyes move to sound; day 14 she "recognizes" her mother; day 18 she makes sounds and turns her head to sound; day 24 she has a sound vocabulary and her mouth will twitch when her mother speaks.

What you can do to help
■ "Answer" all her signals and sounds. Let her see your mouth moving, nod your head and body a lot in greeting;
■ She can see clearly at 8 to 10 inches away so bring your face, colours, or moving fingers into focus for her at this distance.

Stimulate her senses
Talk and sing to her, hold her close and rock her, show her things quite close to her face so she can see them.

4 WEEKS OLD

Your baby understands the mechanics of conversation and opens and closes his mouth in imitation of speech. He will adjust his behaviour to the sound of your voice; he will quieten when you speak soothingly and become distressed if you use rough or loud tones.

What you can do to help
■ Feed his sense of rhythm by speaking in a sing-song fashion. Sing lullabies;
■ Laugh a lot;
■ Be physical. Hold him firmly but rock, sway and turn around. Use a rocking chair or cradle.

Appeal to his love of rhythm
Speak to him in a sing-song voice, sing lullabies to him, and move around rocking and swaying while you hold him.

6 WEEKS OLD

Your baby will smile at you briefly and will bob her head when you talk to her. She will make small, throaty noises when she is spoken to.

What you can do to help
■ She will be concentrating on you, so help her by animating your face and maintaining eye contact whenever you can;
■ To capture her interest, move your fingers and/or toys in and out of her line of vision. Speak alternately at each side.

Awaken her interest
Keep eye contact and make your face interesting when you talk; speak to one side so sounds come from different directions.

MENTAL DEVELOPMENT

8 WEEKS OLD

Your baby smiles readily now and often. He shows interest in his surroundings by looking at the direction of sounds and movements, and stares steadily at objects, as though "grasping with his eyes."

What you can do to help
■ *Add interest to his surroundings by gently propping him up with cushions and surrounding him with a variety of coloured objects;*
■ *Put a mobile and mirror in his bed or pram and offer him a variety of small, soft toys;*
■ *Sing nursery rhymes;*
■ *Show him his hands.*

Make his surroundings of interest
Prop him up so he can look around and see a variety of brightly coloured items that you have strewn around.

12 WEEKS OLD

Your baby is beginning to understand her own body and looks at and moves her fingers at will. She will respond to conversation with a variety of nods, smiles, mouth movements, noises, squeals, and other expressions of delight. She will also make excited movements of her body.

What you can do to help
■ *Respond to all your baby's behaviour with a theatrical, larger-than-life reaction;*
■ *Act out nursery rhymes;*
■ *Play simple physical games — gentle jerks, knee bends, arm pulls, tickling feet;*
■ *Give her small, firm toys of differing weights and textures that can be grasped, handled and felt.*

Show obvious delight
Reward all your baby's behaviour — movements, gestures, and expressions — by over-reacting with praise.

16 WEEKS OLD

Your baby's curiosity is obvious. He is interested in new toys, new sounds, new places, new people, and new sensations. He also recognizes familiar objects and places, and understands routines. He gets excited at the sight of a breast or bottle, and is beginning to reveal a sense of humour. He likes to be able to look around propped up.

What you can do to help
■ *Encourage his sense of humor by following up things your baby finds amusing, laughing with him and sharing jokes;*
■ *Toys will teach your baby about many different things so offer him a wide range that are of differing sizes, shapes, and textures, and that are used differently. Make sure some make noise.*

Feed his curiosity
Amplify his experiences by talking to him about what you see and do. Add as much detail about each object or activity as you can.

20 WEEKS OLD

Your baby loves games, including splashing in the bath. She exhibits developing concentration by spending more time examining things. She smiles at herself in the mirror, turns her head to sounds, and starts to move her arms and legs to attract attention. She pats her bottle.

What you can do to help
■ *So she will learn requests will be answered, and you are the source of help and comfort, respond when she tries to attract your attention with sound, turning your body, making eye contact, and moving towards her;*
■ *Make sure to introduce all strangers to your child;*
■ *Use her name whenever you can.*

Play as many games as you can
"Peek-A-Boo" and "This Little Piggy" are games that she will enjoy. Laugh with her as much as you can.

24 WEEKS OLD

Your baby will make attention-seeking noises and other vocalizations, gets excited when he hears someone coming, and starts to raise his arms to be picked up. He will speak and smile to his mirror image, and blow bubbles. He starts to act shyly with strangers, may exhibit fear, and prefers or dislikes some foods.

What you can do to help
■ *Play dropping an object and giving it back and other give-and-take games;*
■ *Use his name over and over;*
■ *To help him gain a sense of purpose for making things happen and change, demonstrate actions and their results. For example, push a ball and tell him it rolls.*

Respond to attention-seeking
When your baby shows he wants you, go to him holding out your arms; call his name, and let him know you are coming.

28 WEEKS OLD

Your baby will be starting off conversations, and many recognizable sounds should be heard. She knows her own name, puts her arms out to be picked up, and shows her independence by wanting to feed herself. She is starting to imitate simple things and anticipates repetition.

What you can do to help
■ *Show your baby her reflection in the mirror and say her name so that she gains a concept of self. Stress "that's Susan, that's you"(as opposed to I, me). Say "NO" to demonstrate the negative;*
■ *Repeat all the sounds your baby makes likes "ba," "da," and "ka;"*
■ *Encourage self-feeding with finger foods.*

Foster her sense of self
Show your baby her reflection in a mirror. Point to it and say her name aloud. Use her name as often as possible.

MENTAL DEVELOPMENT

32 WEEKS OLD

Your baby is beginning to understand the meaning of words, and knows what "NO" means. He starts to show signs of determination, as in going for toys that are out of reach. Your baby takes a keen interest in games, and concentrates deeply on his toys. He will look around for a dropped toy.

What you can do to help
■ *Play lots of water games. Give him pots, jars, and jugs that he can use to pour, empty, and fill;*
■ *Put his toys just out of reach and retrieve them when he asks;*
■ *Introduce lots of games involving the body such as "Pat-A-Cake;"*
■ *Encourage independence with self-feeding.*

Play lots of water games
Various household items, as well as purpose–made toys, will provide scope for many different activities in the bath.

36 WEEKS OLD

Your baby recognizes familiar games and rhymes, laughs in appropriate parts, and can anticipate movements. She will turn her head to her name, hold out her hands to be washed, but turns her head away from a flannel.

What you can do to help
■ *Impress routines on your baby so she understands life on a day-to-day basis. Explain what you're doing — "Lunch time. First we put on your bib, then you sit in your chair, then Mummy gets your lunch, mm, lovely lunch …;"*
■ *Get noisy toys and/or allow your child to play with safe kitchen utensils.*

Always explain your routines
Use meals, bathtime, or bedtime to explain routines to your child so she gets used to life on a day-to-day basis.

40 WEEKS OLD

Your child is becoming familiar with routines — waving bye-bye, and putting up his foot for a sock, for instance. He knows what a doll or teddy is, and will pat it. He will remember "Pat-A-Cake" all the way through. He will look round corners for a toy, and for Daddy, if you say "Where's Daddy?".

What you can do to help
■ *Provide him with squeaking toys, horns and bells;*
■ *Give him a soft doll "like baby," and show him how to dress and undress it;*
■ *Play drop and pick up games, hide and seek with a toy (to stretch his memory), and "Peek-A-Boo;"*
■ *Show him how to put things in and out of containers.*

Start looking at books together
Choose soft baby books with large bright illustrations, and set aside a quiet time each day, such as bedtime, for "reading."

44 WEEKS OLD

Your child can say one under-standable word. She may show you things in a book but won't concentrate for long. She is constantly dropping toys out of her pram, looking for them, and asking for them to be picked up. She's beginning to understand in and out, here and there.

What you can do to help
■ *Read different kinds of books and magazines;*
■ *Try to increase her concentration by telling her a simple, short story about something that you look at*
■ *play "Pat-A-Cake" and show her how to clap;*
■ *Keep demonstrating cause and effect. Knock over a column of bricks, and say "All fall down."*

Point out items
Name several items on a page in a book or magazine. Take your baby's hand and point to objects, name them, and repeat.

48 WEEKS OLD

Your baby has an intense interest in books and things on pages and likes to have items pointed out. He will repeat his name. He loves jokes and will do anything for a laugh, such as repeating tricks that make you laugh. He will shake his head for "NO."

What you can do to help
■ *Concentrate on the names of objects and the parts of the body. Go over them repeatedly. Do actions so your baby can imitate you. Praise and reward all overtures and responses;*
■ *Tell "stories" to set scenes and create scenarios; describe routines so your baby relates to his world.*

Help your baby imitate you
Point to your nose. Say "This is Mummy's nose." Take his finger, point it at his nose and say "This is Tommy's nose."

1 YEAR OLD

Your baby knows all about kissing and shows an expand-ing repertoire of emotions. He will pick up a doll, hand it to you, and release it. He says two or three words with meaning, may recognize an object in a book and point to it. He starts to understand simple questions.

What you can do to help
■ *To stimulate imagination and the formation of abstract ideas, start reading short stories;*
■ *Encourage showing affection; have him pat doll, stroke dog, kiss Mummy, put arms around Daddy;*
■ *Describe your actions while you demonstrate things like putting on his socks, taking off his coat.*

Read simple stories
Stories about mother and baby animals are pleasing to children, and help them to learn about the sounds animals make.

MENTAL DEVELOPMENT

15 MONTHS OLD

Your toddler knows parts of his body, some objects in a book, can make animal sounds, and will try to take off his clothes, if asked. He will fetch and carry simple things. He has acquired the concept of "cattiness," i.e. he knows that a picture of a cat, a toy cat and a real cat are all cats.

What you can do to help
■ *Give him small, simple tasks to stimulate adventurousness and a sense of achievement. Encourage him to help you with chores such as tidying up and putting things away in the right places;*
■ *Help him to string words together to make simple sentences using three or four words;*
■ *Introduce the concept of possession — "That's Martin's ball, your ball."*

Work towards achievement
Let him help you as much as he can. Simple tasks like tidying up are well within his abilities and encourage feelings of pride.

18 MONTHS OLD

Your toddler can recognize a few items on a page and will point to them if you say their names. She may attempt a few chores, and will try to imitate your actions. She can carry out a request that requires assessment and memory — "Go and bring me your teddy."

What you can do to help
■ *Language development depends on memory and understanding. Encourage learning through repetition and talk her through situations "Now where is it? In the bathroom. There it is. Pick it up;"*
■ *Introduce the possessive pronoun. "This is my apple, that is your apple;"*
■ *Introduce your child to shapes with a simple form board.*

Use repetition for learning
Whenever you do something repeat certain key phrases over and over. "Sophie has an apple. Yes, Sophie has an apple."

21 MONTHS OLD

Your toddler can ask for food, drink, toys, and about going to the potty. He can carry out several simple requests and is beginning to understand more complicated ones —"Please get your hairbrush from the bathroom." He may grab your arm or use other gestures to get your attention.

What you can do to help
■ *Describe the properties of everything, e.g. birds and planes fly, cars go "brrm," glue is sticky, fur is soft, balls are round and roll, bricks are square and can't roll;*
■ *Describe the colour of everything;*
■ *Introduce opposites such as rough and smooth;*
■ *Start to use numbers. Demonstrate with your fingers, then use your baby's fingers.*

Describe the properties of things
When showing something to your child, point out whether it is hard or soft, its colour, if it makes noise, its sounds, etc.

2 YEARS OLD

Your child has a rapidly increasing vocabulary of names and objects, and can describe the properties of familiar items and identify them. She can obey complicated orders, and will find an object played with previously. She talks non-stop, and asks occasional questions.

What you can do to help
■ *Show her how to use simple tools such as a spade or hammer;*
■ *Introduce your child to other children but don't force her to play with them;*
■ *Give her pencils and paints and encourage her drawing;*
■ *Read longer, more complicated stories and fairy tales;*
■ *Keep musical interest going with sing-alongs and music and story cassettes.*

Stimulate spatial intelligence
Help her place the various cubes, rectangles and squares into their correct receptacles in a shape-fitting toy or box.

2 ½ YEARS OLD

Your child starts to add detail to broad concepts, e.g. a horse has a long tail. He knows one or two nursery rhymes and can find them in his book, more colours, a few numbers, and can count, perhaps to three. He knows his name. He starts to ask "why" and says "no," "won't," "can't."

What you can do to help
■ *Provide a toy set of many pieces, e.g. a farm yard, and use it to count cows, sheep, pigs, and chickens;*
■ *Encourage him to draw familiar objects and note increasing detail. Describe them and add more detail. Give all drawing and painting interest full outlet;*
■ *Talk over incidents and experiences to strengthen memory.*

Play lots of number games
Incorporate numbers into everything you do. Count items when you shop, get dressed, or say what you have to do.

3 YEARS OLD

Your child asks questions incessantly "What?", "Where?", "How", "Why?". She can count to ten, and build complicated structures with blocks. She can dress her doll, and likes "real-life" games. She has a good memory and refers to the past. She knows her own gender.

What you can do to help
■ *Work on her memory by reminding her of what you did before. "We went to the supermarket yesterday, remember?";*
■ *When she finds something difficult say, "I can help you to do that," and demonstrate;*
■ *Make up stories with your child as the main character;*
■ *Increase the number of books and stories you read.*

Add to her sense of self
Encourage independence and self-reliance by involving your child in simple decisions: ask her to choose her clothes and food.

LOCOMOTION

Strange as it may seem, learning to walk, run, skip, and jump begins with your child being able to control his or her head. Therefore, when your child's head begins to lift at four weeks of age, you are observing your baby's first efforts to walk. As with all development, progress proceeds from head to toe, so head control is the essential first phase.

During these first weeks, your baby's legs and arms will start to take up more mature positions – all steps in achieving successful locomotion. Then, in readily perceivable stages, your baby will use the arms and legs to make more and more refined and coordinated movements as the muscles strengthen. These movements will first enable your child to sit erect, then crawl, stand, and walk.

Before some babies learn to walk, however, they may learn to move from place to place by a variety of other methods. Some become proficient at getting about by rolling; others may progress by a series of bumps on the buttocks; still others may get about on one hand and buttock, or both hands and both buttocks; and some may crawl backwards. Once your child's mastered the basics of locomotion, he will then refine them until he can run, skip, and jump gracefully, and skate, ride a bike and climb with ease. Throughout this process, you can help by performing the exercises and playing the games set out in the charts. These are meant to be fun and should be fitted in whenever you have the time and your child is in a receptive mood.

PROVIDING A SAFE ENVIRONMENT

Once your child starts to move around easily, your main concern will be to keep him safe. The following guidelines should be followed:

☐ Block open stairways and other unsafe areas with gates. These should be made of a rigid mesh with a straight top edge and should be swung open from a fixed surround. (Wooden, expandable gates with diamond-shaped openings are dangerous). Gates that rely on pressure should not be used where there is any possibility they could fall – like the top of a stairway. The

pressure bar must be fixed on the sideaway from the child.
□ The home is filled with hazardous items for young children. In addition to poisonous substances in the bathroom and kitchen, many houseplants àre dangerous to young children. The kitchen also contains many appliances with long cords, sharp implements, foil and plastic wrap packages with sharp edges, hot liquids, etc. Children should never be allowed to roam free in the kitchen. □ Baby walkers should conform to standards of safety and should only be used under supervision. Never allow your child to use a walker near a cooker, fireplace, heater or other heat source. To minimize accidents, check that floor surfaces are flat and free of obstacles, including rug edges and raised thresholds.

□ Outside play equipment should be firmly anchored in the ground by concrete at the base of the supports. The concrete should be covered with cushioning material. Avoid treating wooden equipment with wood preservatives that contain creosote or pentachlorophenol. Once your child starts riding a bike, using a skateboard or skates, encourage him to wear a helmet and padding.

LOCOMOTION

NEWBORN

Certain postures are typical of the newborn. She will turn her head to a preferred side, whether she is placed on her back or stomach, and will flex her limbs into her body.

What you can do to help
■ *To enable your baby to take up more mature positions, do gentle leg exercises that will bend and straighten her legs;*
■ *The relative largeness of your baby's head, approximately one-fourth of her entire length, is too heavy for her back and neck muscles to lift. Strengthen her muscles so her neck will stiffen by holding her in a face-down positiontwo to three times a day.*

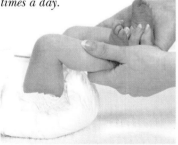

Ease her out of fetal positions
Do gentle knee bends and straighten her legs gently during nappy-changing times, which will accelerate your baby's adopting positions other than fetal ones.

4 WEEKS OLD

Your baby still has little strength in his neck muscles; his head will lag unless it is supported. If lying prone, he can lift his chin off the bed for a few seconds, and if held in a sitting position, he may hold up his head for a moment.

What you can do to help
■ *Continue as for a newborn;*
■ *Move your fingers, or a toy or other object, up through your baby's field of vision to encourage him to move his head.*

Give him something to look at
While he is lying prone, move your fingers upwards or pull a coloured object through his field of vision, so that his eyes and head follow your movements.

6 WEEKS OLD

Your baby can raise her face 45 degrees to her bed, show much less head lag when she is pulled to sit, and hold her head in line with her body for a few minutes when held face down. Her knees and hips are becoming stronger and not so flexed as before.

What you can do to help
■ *So that your baby has to lift her head to see them, put bright objects in front of her head;*
■ *To strengthen the whole of her legs, play leg-stretching games at nappy-changing times.*

Encourage her to lift her head
When your baby is lying down, take a brightly coloured toy and hold it close to your baby's head, but enough off the surface so that she has to raise her head to see it.

8 WEEKS OLD

Your baby can hold his head up, while in a standing or sitting position, or while lying prone, but not for very long. When he is held in a prone position, he can hold his head in line with his body.

What you can do to help

■ *To teach your baby about balance, which he perceives in the ear, brain, spine, and muscles, make a game of holding him in a standing position;*
■ *So he will take interest in his surroundings, prop your baby up in a seat, and introduce him to some soft, brightly coloured articles.*

Provide items to reach for
Prop your baby up in his seat or against some pillows and, to encourage him to take swipes at some soft, coloured articles, put a variety close by.

12 WEEKS OLD

Your baby can keep her head held up constantly now when lying prone, and if pulled into a sitting position, or kept propped up, her head will lag hardly at all.

What you can do to help

■ *To strengthen your baby's neck and shoulder muscles further, occasionally play at pulling her into a sitting position when she is lying on her back;*
■ *To encourage her to reach out, place soft objects in front of her when she's lying down. During this manoeuvre, she will learn to put her weight on one arm while reaching out with the other hand.*

Muscle-strengthening games
Play with your baby by laying her down and then gently pulling her into a sitting position. Look into her eyes, and say "Peek-A-Boo." Repeat this as much as you like.

16 WEEKS OLD

Your baby loves sitting up now and looking around, but he needs support; his head will lag momentarily when he is pulled to sit. He can keep his head held up, though it will still wobble if he moves suddenly, and if lying down, he can look straight at you.

What you can do to help

■ *To strengthen the muscles of your baby's trunk, play games that make him swivel;*
■ *To encourage independent balance and maximum movements, offer him a few soft toys for which he has to reach out;*
■ *Sit him in a chair with good support, using cushions, if necessary.*

Encourage balance
Add a new dimension to playing "Peek-A-Boo" by staying slightly to your baby's side when you call to him so he has to swing his trunk to find you.

LOCOMOTION

20 WEEKS OLD

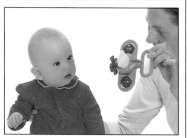

Your baby now has full head control. Even when she is pulled into a sitting position, or when she rocks about, her head will not lag.

What you can do to help
◼ *In order for your baby to walk, her head must be entirely stable. To help her progress properly, give her plenty of rocking exercises.*

Play for stablilizing her head
Rock your baby frequently. This will give her plenty of practice in keeping her head stable. You can dance gently around the room with her or swing her in your arms.

24 WEEKS OLD

Your baby's muscles have strengthened enough so that he can put a lot of his weight on his forearms; he sits with hands forward for support. He can hold his hands out to be lifted, and sit supported on his own for a few minutes in a highchair.

What you can do to help
◼ *To strengthen bones and muscles preparatory to walking, play bouncing games with your baby;*
◼ *To encourage him to pull his tummy off the floor in preparation for crawling, play at airplanes: Lay side-by-side on your abdomens and lift both your arms and torsos off the floor;*
◼ *Reward him for holding out his arms by playing lifting games.*

Weight-bearing exercises
With your baby on your lap, gently bounce him up and down. This is good practice for helping him to take more and more of his own weight preparatory to walking.

28 WEEKS OLD

Your baby now can bear weight on one hand in a prone position, sit without support, lift her head spontaneously when lying on her back, and take all her own weight on straight knees and hips when you hold her up.

What you can do to help
◼ *To get your baby to lift her head, while your baby is lying down, offer her some toys just out of reach;*
◼ *To get your baby to take all her own weight, encourage all standing games.*

Encourage head lift
With your baby lying on her back, hold up some brightly coloured or noisy toys just out of her reach. She'll be encouraged to lift up her head to have a look.

32 WEEKS OLD

Your baby may try to move; he will stretch out and reach for a toy. He may rock his body back and forth. His hips and knees are stronger and he will relish taking his own weight by standing. If his arms are held, he will bounce about.

What you can do to help
■ *To encourage him to shuffle along on his bottom, which gives him the sensation of being mobile and encourages self-confidence and independence, sit a short way away from your child, and reach out your arms to him;*
■ *To prepare his legs for walking, play standing and bouncing games holding him on your lap, on a bed, on cushions, or in the bath.*

Getting him to move
Sit a short way away from your baby and reach out your arms to him. Encourage him to come to you by calling his name and offering a toy that he likes.

36 WEEKS OLD

Your baby can take all her weight on her own legs but she needs to hold on to do so. She can sit for 10 minutes, lean forward and sideways, and stay balanced. She may roll over or try to crawl. She finds it very difficult to sit from a standing position.

What you can do to help
■ *Encourage her standing by helping her to stable pieces of furniture and clamping her hands on so she is balanced;*
■ *To get her to lean forward and sideways while maintaining her balance, place toys just out of reach, in front of her and at her side, while she is sitting;*
■ *To make it easier for her to sit froma standing position, bend her hips and knees.*

Let her take her weight
Help your baby to latch on to stable pieces of furniture. Take her over to a sturdy chair or low table, position her hands, and stay close by while she holds on.

40 WEEKS OLD

Your baby is mobile now, and moves forward a little on his hands and knees. He can pull himself up and enjoys changing from sitting to lying positions. His lateral trunk muscles are getting stronger and he begins to twist his trunk around while he sits.

What you can do to help
■ *Offer your fingers so he will be encouraged to pull himself up and to sit and stand. He will be amazed and delighted at his prowess. Praise him well;*
■ *To help him learn stepping, while he is standing up, bend one of his knees and lift his foot from the floor. When he does it, tell him "Clever boy;"*
■ *To make him twist, place a toy behind his back. Support him as he twists around.*

Encourage him to crawl to you
Put your baby on his hands and knees and sit a short distance away. He will come to you if you hold out your arms, call his name, or offer a brightly coloured toy.

LOCOMOTION

Completely mobile while sitting, your baby will be creeping everywhere as well. She will be lifting her foot while she stands.

What you can do to help
■ *Continue as for 40 weeks:*
■ *Put her into a crawl position and encourage her to traverse short distances;*
■ *To help her learn stepping, while she is standing up, bend one of her knees and lift her foot from the floor. When she does it, tell her "Clever girl;"*
■ *To make her twist around, place a toy behind her back where she'll have to turn to reach it. Support her as she twists.*

Help her to stand
Offer her your fingers so that she can pull herself up. Make her feel proud of her achievement by rewarding her with smiles, "Clever girl," and hand claps.

Your baby walks sideways by holding on to furniture; he will walk forward if both hands are held. When sitting down, he can turn around and pick up an object without wobbling.

What you can do to help
■ *Place furniture around the room, only one side-step apart, so your baby can walk sideways and "cruise" around the whole space;*
■ *Help him to practise walking around with you holding only one of his hands.*

Facilitate his cruising
Position stable pieces of furniture so that they are only one side-step apart. Remove all items that can tip over easily. Encourage him to move sideways around the room.

Your baby can walk if you hold only one of her hands. When she crawls she will do so on her hands and feet, in much the same way as a bear does.

What you can do to help
■ *To encourage independent stepping, practise asking your baby to come to you while she is cruising;*
■ *To give her the courage to launch herself off, put your pieces of furniture slightly further apart.*

Encourage her to walk to you
Sit a little way away from your baby while she is holding on to a piece of furniture. Hold out your arms, call her name, and ask her to come to you.

13 MONTHS OLD

Your baby can now stand alone, and may even take her first independent step.

What you can do to help
■ *To make her feel proud of her great achievement, let her know how wonderful you think it is that she can stand, and perhaps take a step alone. Celebrate with her by giving her lots of encouragement;*
■ *To encourage independent standing, provide her with a stable, standing toy for her to hold on to;*
■ *Don't rush her into shoes; she doesn't need any until she begins to walk outside.*

Let her practise standing
Stable toys or pieces of furniture with rounded edges are ideal for holding on to for independent stepping. Once she is mobile watch her at all times.

15 MONTHS OLD

Your child can kneel and lower his body to sit without support; he can stand up, creep upstairs, and walk. His steps are high, unsteady, and of unequal length and direction.

What you can do to help
■ *To encourage him to practise hip and knee bending, get him a special chair with arms that will enable him to sit down by himself without falling;*
■ *Prevent accidents by paying him constant attention while he walks or creeps upstairs;*
■ *Offer him maximum freedom of movement, by putting on reins so he can wander safely;*
■ *To get him to practise leg movements, get a large soft ball and kick it to each other.*

Provide him with a sturdy chair
Your toddler will love getting in and out of a chair; this also will enable him to practise bending and flexing his hips and knees. Choose a chair that will not tip over.

18 MONTHS OLD

Your toddler can climb stairs unaided, both feet on each step, though she needs to hold on. She walks with a steadier, lower-stepping gait, runs, walks backwards, and seldom falls.

What you can do to help
■ *Assist your toddler in mastering hip and knee bends, essential for a range of movements like "proper falling;"*
■ *Get her to practise walking backwards by playing games that use backward steps;*
■ *To encourage a wide range of movements, provide her with pulling and pushing toys;*
■ *To make picking up objects easier, give her support if she bends down from standing;*
■ *Encourage her to kick out by playing gentle football games.*

Exercise hip and knee muscles
Show your toddler how to squat to accelerate her muscles' development. Encourage her to imitate you. Hold on to her hands while playing "Ring-A-Rosy."

LOCOMOTION

21 MONTHS OLD

Your toddler now can pick up objects without falling over. He walks backwards easily; can walk upstairs, both feet on each step, but without holding on, and can stop quickly and turn corners. He also is more fluent at games such as football.

What you can do to help
■ *To encourage the many movements of which he is now capable, get him to join in with most of your activities. Make going upstairs, dancing, washing your face, etc., things he can do along with you.*

Widen his range of activities
Your toddler is fascinated by everything you do and will want to imitate your every move. Use every opportunity to get him to join in your daily activities.

2 YEARS OLD

Your child is starting to get rhythm, and enjoys making movements related to dancing. She can run, but not slow down or turn corners, and can squat down with ease.

What you can do to help
■ *To give her scope for rhythmic movements, dance with her to music; include kneeling and swaying actions, clap hands and sing;*
■ *Don't expect her to run around corners or to stop easily; the muscles that control running and turning still are not strong enough.*

Dance and sing
Making movements to rhythmical music is an activity your child will enjoy, and one that will also give her practice in making a wide range of movements.

2 ½ YEARS OLD

Your child can jump with his feet off the ground, walk on tip toe, is steady enough on his feet to carry a breakable object, and can hold a baby brother or sister on his knee.

What you can do to help
■ *Feed his love of motion and strengthen his muscles at the same time, by providing him with a moving toy he can propel when sitting on it;*
■ *Encourage his agility by playing games involving jumping and walking on tip toe.*

Provide him with a moving toy
Give him a toy with wheels that he will have to sit on, and use his feet to propel. He is probably too young for a bicycle, but many simpler, suitable moving toys are available.

3 YEARS OLD

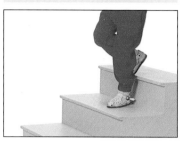

Your child has become much more nimble. She can walk upstairs with one foot on each step, jump off the bottom step, stand on one foot for a second, swing her arms like an adult when walking, and can ride a tricycle.

What you can do to help
■ *Let her practise her jumping by playing hopscotch, or holding hands and hopping on one foot at a time;*
■ *Practise arm swinging by marching to music;*
■ *To strengthen her calf muscles and encourage flexibility in her feet, provide her with a tricycle;*
■ *Encourage physical confidence with mobile toys such as a swing, see-saw, and slide.*

Play hopping games
Your child will enjoy playing jumping games, such as hopscotch, which also are good to work off excess energy. Include hopping in other games such as "Simon Says."

4 YEARS OLD

Your child has become very active and should be well coordinated. He races about hopping, jumping, climbing, and goes downstairs rapidly one foot per step. He even can carry a cup of liquid without spilling any.

What you can do to help
■ *Offer activities that depend on muscle coordination. He should now be able to master skipping rope, and a wide range of other physical games;*
■ *Take him to playgrounds with a wide range of equipment and, if you have a garden or yard, install a climbing frame, outside on the grass, which is stable and provides scope for muscular activities.*

Have him skip rope
All his muscles are working to-gether now, and play such as this gives him a work-out for a wide range of movements. Make sure he has access to outdoor apparatus.

5 YEARS OLD

Your child's coordination is finely developed and she is capable of a great many movements. She can walk a straight line, go down stairs on alternating feet, skip rope using alternate feet, climb confidently, and enjoy quick-moving toys and games.

What you can do to help
■ *Encourage adventurousness by providing skates, a skate board or stilts that will allow her practice in movement; she will probably be able to perform on them for a short time only;*
■ *Take her to playgrounds where she can swing and climb on the apparatus; if you have a garden or yard, install swings, hang ropes from tree branches, and/or build a treehouse.*

Encourage adventurousness
Provide her with toys or other equipment that will challenge her coordination and manoeuvr-ability. Keep her safe by having her wear protective clothing.

MANIPULATION

The primitive infant is born with several involuntary reflexes that have to be unlearned before manipulative skills can be acquired. A newborn infant's grasp reflex, so strong it can bear the weight of the baby, and a holdover from the time we were tree-swinging primates, must be lost before she can voluntarily grasp and hold something. The startle reflex, displayed by all newborns, and manifested as its spreading its fingers out like a star, must be superceded if a child is ever to write with a pencil.

The young baby starts using her mouth as the main organ of touch. Later on, the fingertips take over. Over the first year, she will refine her grasp so that instead of holding a block with the palm of her hand, she will be able to grasp it between thumb and finger. This particular achievement distinguishes us from all other species; no other has such superior manipulative abilities. Another great step forward comes when your baby lets go of an object easily; now the muscles of letting go are learning to work against the muscles of holding so that the two opposing muscle groups are working together.

You can help your baby acquire and perfect these skills – which are used everyday in feeding, dressing, and play – and which are necessary if she is to become independent, by performing the activities in the chart.

The young baby grasps a cube in his palm.

The older child is capable of precise use of thumb and fingers.

A word about handling genitals

Babies usually become aware of their genital organs toward the end of the first year but handle them without any obvious pleasure. Handling eventually does bring a pleasurable sensation, becoming more like real masturbation. Most children of both sexes masturbate, and it is perfectly normal behaviour. Fondling their genitals will not cause children to become blind, insane or homosexual. There is no reason to discourage it or to show disapproval, for then the child will grow guilty and secretive. If masturbation occurs in public, the best way to deal with it is to distract the child, rather than to scold or show disapproval.

"Train without smokestack": At around 2½ years of age your child may make this structure if you show her how.

Towers: Until your child is at least 18 months old, he will not be able to stack 3 or 4 bricks. Only by 2 to 2½ years can your child successfully attempt a tower of between 4 and 8 blocks.

"Train with a smokestack": This is not within your child's capabilities to imitate until he is 2½ years or older.

Tower of 9 or 10 bricks: Around 3 years of age your child may be able to master the tall tower.

Building Blocks
Great toys for all ages, use them, too, to assess your child's development.

"Bridge": Your child will not have enough dexterity to build this until at least 3½ years old.

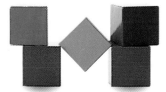

"Gate": Around 4½ years your child should be able to tackle more complex structures, once you've shown her how.

MANIPULATION

NEWBORN	4 WEEKS OLD	6 WEEKS OLD
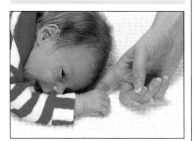		

NEWBORN

Your baby keeps her hands tightly closed most of the time; due to her "grasp" reflex she will hold on tightly to a finger. However, when your baby is disturbed, by a sudden loud noise or violent movement, she will spread out her fingers in the "startle" reflex.

What you can do to help

■ *Your baby will have to lose the grasp reflex before she can voluntarily hold on to something. You can test to see how the reflex fades by letting her hold on to your forefingers, and see how far you can pull them off the mattress.*

Test her grasp reflex
Let her hold on to your forefingers and see how high you can pull them off the mattress. Over the first few weeks, her grasp will weaken.

4 WEEKS OLD

Your baby's grasp reflex is fading but he still keeps his hands closed up.

What you can do to help

■ *To encourage his fingers to relax, play games during which you can unfold his fingers one at a time, like "This Little Piggy."*

Open fingers one at a time
Play games like "This Little Piggy," during which you can open out and separate his fingers. You can do the same with his toes.

6 WEEKS OLD

Your baby's grasp reflex has almost completely gone. Her hands are held open most of the time.

What you can do to help

■ *Make your baby aware of her hands; continue to play "This Little Piggy," but also tickle the palm of her hand and her fingertips with anything soft and furry; massage and rub her hands gently, too.*

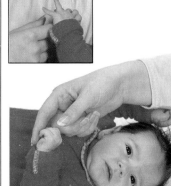

Make her aware of her hands
Gently massage and tickle your baby's hands and fingers. Rub or brush across them with materials of different textures, if possible.

8 WEEKS OLD

Your baby's hands are becoming much more loosely open and he is starting to become aware of them.

What you can do to help

■ *Increase his awareness of his hands by using all kinds of tactile stimulation. Objects of different textures are good;*

■ *When you place something in your baby's palm, lay it across (not down) following his palmar creases. Bear in mind that your baby's finger-tips are the most sensitive part of his hand, though at first he is going to hold things by clasping them in his palm and bringing his fingers straight down.*

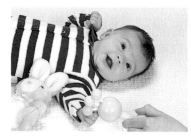

Increase awareness of his hands
Let your baby touch toys or objects of different textures, temperatures, and materials. Water, baby powder, and warm skin are good, too.

12 WEEKS OLD

Your baby's grasp reflex has disappeared. She mainly keeps her hands open and will look at them. She will hold a rattle if it is placed in her hand, and even retain it for a few minutes. She looks as though she wants to grasp.

What you can do to help

■ *To encourage a mature grasp, give her a rattle;*

■ *Play with her fingers while she's lying on her back, and she can study them;*

■ *Give her something to look at and reach for. Put a mobile above her bed and a baby "gym" across her bed or pram to take swipes at;*

■ *Keep having her experience different sensations — splash her hands in her bath, and offer toys of different textures.*

Give her something to hold
Place a rattle in her hand and shake it a few times. She will be intrigued by its texture and the sounds it makes.

16 WEEKS OLD

Your baby is getting his hands and feet under control: he moves his hands and feet together, puts his foot on his opposite knee, places his soles on his mattress. He shakes a rattle but cannot pick it up. He will pull his clothes over his face in play.

What you can do to help

■ *Make him reach for things by presenting him with interesting objects while he is lying down or sitting propped up;*

■ *Compensate for any overshooting by ensuring he gets the object; laugh at his successes and he'll laugh with you and be pleased;*

■ *To encourage him to make noises with his hand, give him different kinds of rattles.*

Show him interesting objects
Offer him different objects so he will be encouraged to reach for them. He will probably overshoot, so put them in his hands.

43

MANIPULATION

20 WEEKS OLD

Your baby has found her toes, and can put her fist in her mouth. In fact, she will put everything in her mouth. She will reach for large objects with both hands, and will grasp objects on the little finger side of her palm. Your baby will grasp everything within reach. She loves crumpling paper.

What you can do to help
■ *To encourage her to open her fingers and let go, play giving and taking away games;*
■ *Foster her knowledge of her toes by putting them in her mouth, and by playing with them where she can see, as in "This Little Piggy;"*
■ *Give her tissue paper to play with.*

Practise giving and taking away
Play at putting something in her hand, and then opening her fingers and removing it. She will reach for a bottle to feed herself; try and get her to give it back to you.

24 WEEKS OLD

Your baby's movements have become more refined and he is able just to transfer an object from one hand to the other. If he has an object in his hand, he will drop it to pick up another. He can hold his bottle and can grasp.

What you can do to help
■ *To encourage finer finger movements, present him with a variety of finger foods;*
■ *To refine his grasp, start teaching him to eat with a spoon by himself;*
■ *Show him how to pass an object from hand to hand.*

Start him on finger foods
Biscuits, rusks, soft wholemeal bread fingers without crusts or coverings, and cheese cubes are ideal foods for easy grasping and self feeding.

28 WEEKS OLD

Your baby can grasp an object more precisely, and reaches for it with her fingers. She can transfer an object from one hand to another easily, retains an object if she reaches for another, bangs the table with her toys, and is becoming more accurate when she feeds herself with a spoon. She can feed herself with simple finger foods like a biscuit.

What you can do to help
■ *Initiate self-feeding by leaving her alone with food in a dish. Let her start by using her fingers and then finish off with a spoon. Give lots of finger foods;*
■ *To encourage a mature grasp, make cheese cubes smaller and smaller, as small as your baby can manage.*

Continue with self feeding
Leave your baby to progress at her own pace. Put her food in a dish with a spoon by its side, and let her get on with it. She may eat with her fingers or use her spoon.

32 WEEKS OLD

Your baby enjoys making noise by banging his toys. He has refined his movements so that he can tear up paper. Your baby will hold an object firmly in his fingers.

What you can do to help
■ *Feed his love of making noise by giving him spoons, pot lids, or a toy drum to bang;*
■ *Teach him to pick up a brick and try to put it on top of another. He can build a tower of 2 bricks.*

Give him something to bang
Provide him with an array of wooden spoons, metal pots, pans and lids, or a toy drum or other instrument with which to make lots of different sounds.

36 WEEKS OLD

Your baby's movements are becoming more refined and mouthing is decreasing. She can start to point with her index finger, she can lean forward and pick up small things easily, and she can bring two blocks together as though comparing one to the other. She may be able to pick up something as small as a pea with her fingers and thumb, or may try to.

What you can do to help
■ *Show your baby that bricks are of the same size and volume by stacking one exactly on top of another, and side by side;*
■ *Play pointing games such as a simple version of "I Spy;"*
■ *Make at least one meal a day that contains small pieces of food she can pick up.*

Encourage her to build
Stack blocks or cubes of the same size one on top of another and side by side for her to see. However, she is not yet ready to build even a small tower.

40 WEEKS OLD

Your baby can pick up something small by bringing his thumb and index finger together – a great achievement. He goes for objects with his index finger, and can let go of things deliberately. Your child is nearly able to build a tower of 2 blocks, and will actively investigate noisy toys, such as poking at a clapper in a bell.

What you can do to help
■ *Give him practice in letting go by putting lots of toys in his grasp so he can throw them out. Tie them to the sides of his pushchair, if you like. Reward him with approval when he lets go;*
■ *Encourage him to roll a ball to you. When he is sitting, roll it between his legs so he can catch it.*

Demonstate movements
Show him how to put in and take out small objects to and from a container. Show him your approval when he imitates you.

MANIPULATION

Your baby is able to let go of objects easily, and she can spend long periods putting things into and taking them out of containers. She will hold something out to you if you reach for it, and likes to play clapping games such as "Pat-A-Cake."

What you can do to help
■ *Learning to let go of objects easily is a complicated manoeuvre for the brain to master and control, and needs lots of practice. Provide lots of small objects to put in and take out of containers;*
■ *Play giving things to each other and then taking things away gently, without forcing her to relinquish them;*
■ *Play repetitive rhythmic swinging games.*

Provide practice in letting go
Give her cans and a box, bricks and a basket, wooden spoons and a plastic bowl, to practise putting in and taking out.

Your baby now is able to throw things deliberately. He has stopped putting everything in his mouth. He also tries to hold on to two blocks in one of his hands.

What you can do to help
■ *To give him practice holding more than one block, keep putting two into one of his hands;*
■ *Encourage him to eat more of his food with a spoon.*

Give him two blocks to hold
Let him get used to the sensation of having more than one block to hold on to although he will still continue to drop one or both.

Your baby feeds herself more and more and spills less of her food. She can rotate her hand to get the food to her mouth. She enjoys throwing things, can make lines with a pencil, and can hold two blocks in her hand. Having mastered releasing objects, she can build a tower of two blocks.

What you can do to help
■ *To avoid the demoralization of spills, give her only semi-runny food to eat by herself;*
■ *Give her a stubby pencil or crayon to hold on to, and lots of cheap paper to scribble on; display her pictures where she can see them.*

Offer food to eat with a spoon
If you give her more solid food that sticks to the spoon, and doesn't slide off so easily, she will be encouraged to feed herself.

15 MONTHS OLD

Your toddler can pick up and hold a cup, drink from it, and put it down without spilling much. She can feed herself with a spoon, and get it to her mouth before anything runs off. She can build a tower of 3 blocks, tries to turn over the pages of a book, and to put on some of her clothes herself.

What you can do to help
■ *Give her plenty of practice in building towers;*
■ *Supply her with board books, and show her how to turn over the pages;*
■ *Be patient when she tries to dress herself and show her how to put on socks, shoes or a hat;*
■ *Make music together on simple instruments — a tambourine, drum, toy piano.*

Spend time building towers
Your toddler can now manage putting 3 blocks, one on top of another. To increase her dexterity, practise building towers with her.

18 MONTHS OLD

Among a variety of finer movements, your toddler can turn over two to three pages of a book at a time, and is fascinated by zips and other fastenings. She can feed herself completely, including using a cup without spilling anything. She also enjoys finger painting and making scribbles.

What you can do to help
■ *Twisting is a hard movement for the brain and muscles to master, so give her plenty of practice with items that require fine finger movements, such as an activity board with all kinds of devices including knobs, levers, and dials for the bath or nursery, and/or a book with buttons, zips, velcro, and press studs;*
■ *Give her plenty of paper and colour pencils or crayons.*

Give her objects to manipulate
Turning, twisting, spinning, dialling and sliding movements, all require practice provided by an activity board or other similar toy.

2 YEARS OLD

Your child can now turn over the pages of a book, one at a time, and can put on her socks, shoes and gloves. She can turn a knob to open a door, unscrew loose lids from jars, undo and do up a zip, and can propel a pencil more deliberately. She can build a tower 4 cubes high.

What you can do to help
■ *Self-dressing incorporates a range of fine movements especially if clothes have buttons, press studs or zips. Let her choose her own clothes and practise getting dressed and undressed. However, don't dress your child in zippered trousers yet;*
■ *Further practice for tiny muscles can be provided by toys that need to be fitted together, such as Lego.*

Encourage her to dress herself
You will give your child plenty of scope for fine finger movements if you let her dress and undress herself as much as she can.

MANIPULATION

2 ½ YEARS OLD

Your child can thread beads and fasten an easily placed button into a slack buttonhole. He can, therefore, put on and take off trousers, pants and vests, and the occasional shirt. His drawings are more representational and he can build a tower 8 blocks high.

What you can do to help
■ *Encourage your child to make more complicated structures out of construction toys;*
■ *Invest in an easel and furnish it with lots of paper, and all kinds of drawing and colouring materials.*

Stimulate finer movements
Give him blocks and other toys to build more complicated models, which require pressing and fitting pieces together, and use the small muscles of the hand.

3 YEARS OLD

Your child can draw a recognizable image, fasten and unfasten buttons by herself, so she can dress and undress herself completely, if she wishes. She can build a tower 9 blocks high. She is also starting to try and use scissors — a huge step forward in brain/muscle coordination, and in manual dexterity.

What you can do to help
■ *Give your child tasks that require a degree of flexibility;*
■ *Give your child complicated shapes to paint; see that she keeps the outline tidy;*
■ *Introduce simple models and crafts to make;*
■ *Show her how to make up games with finger puppets.*

Putting dexterity to work
Have your child help with simple tasks that involve a number of coordinated movements, like setting the table.

4 YEARS OLD

Your child can copy a circle very well if you show him how. He can also copy two straight lines crossing at right angles, though imperfectly. He's getting much better at fine tasks, e.g. setting the table properly, washing his face and hands, making his bed, and putting his clothes tidily away.

What you can do to help
■ *Draw a simple picture, and ask your child to cut it into pieces and fit them together again like a jigsaw;*
■ *Do simple jigsaws together;*
■ *Point out your child's name and let him try to copy it if he wants to, in preparation for the pencil control needed for writing;*
■ *Draw an incomplete man and ask your child to complete it (see p 112).*

Facilitate small movements
Placing small objects close together is now within your child's abilities and requires practice to perfect. Give him small toys to arrange.

SOCIABILITY

When babies arrive in the world they are formidably equipped to interact with parents; they possess the socializing instincts to make a parent want to receive as well as give messages. In other words, both parent and newborn are ready for the two-way intercourse that underlies all social interaction. In contrast, the baby's involvement with toys is a one-sided affair, and the baby knows it. Toys can please him, but toys can't be pleased. There is no feedback to nurture a warm, on-going relationship. Babies seek out a caring interest, and only people give it and only people, particularly parents with their own brand of loving interest, can make a baby a social being.

This seeking responsiveness from others is evident in all babies, and if we wish our children to grow up into open, loving adults we must service their demands from the very outset and respond to them. In doing so, we make them responsive to others, friendly, outgoing, and affectionate, so we serve them well because they are welcomed and loved by others. The relationship a child forms with its parents, and in the first instance with its mother, is the blueprint for all other relationships. Babies become social by imitating us. They first imitate facial expresions then gestures, then movements, then whole patterns of behaviour. In as short a time as the first year, many basic social rituals have been picked up and learned from parents, who therefore have the responsibility to be more socially aware than they have ever been. Babies respond to high-pitched human voices from the moment of birth, at which time you should start talking and never stop. Starting to talk to your baby starts her off on the path to sociability.

SOCIABILITY

NEWBORN

Your baby wants to listen, look, and respond to your overtures. She nods, bobs, makes mouth movements, protrudes her tongue, and jerks her body.

What you can do to help
■ *Make sure your baby has frequent contact with your skin as this is critical for establishing social bonding;*
■ *Get a two–way "conversation" going by answering all her responses. This will encourage her to "talk" back.*

Establishing bonding
Babies are responsive to nurturing right away. Bonding relies on eye-to-eye and skin-to-skin contact.

12 WEEKS OLD

Your baby will turn her head to your voice, and smile in welcome. She expresses pleasure by smiling, kicking her legs, and waving her arms.

What you can do to help
■ *Many of your child's first impressions of the world are through feeding – bottle or breast. Make eye contact so she experiences social contact along with the pleasurable sensation of being fed;*
■ *Your baby will learn that being friendly is rewarding if you respond with interest, love, cuddles, comfort and soothing noises. A child who is smiled at smiles back, and smiles in greeting.*

Make eye contact while feeding
Make feeding into a time of physical intimacy; hold her close, look into her eyes, and talk gently.

16 WEEKS OLD

Your baby will look at, and smile at, people who speak to or play with him. He knows you, and other members of his family. He doesn't like being alone with a toy for too long, and cries when he's left by himself. He will stop crying if you go to him, and wriggles his body in anticipation.

What you can do to help
■ *Turn and face your baby in a theatrical manner so he can see easily you are attending to him. Make eye contact as often as possible, and exaggerate all facial expressions and gestures;*
■ *Imitate everything your baby does, but overly so;*
■ *Spend as much time playing with him as you can. Singing and rhythmic games will encourage him to make sounds back.*

Overact your responses
Use large and exaggerated gestures when you respond so he can see easily you are attending to him.

20 WEEKS OLD

Your baby exhibits shyness by turning her face and body away, but will smile at familiar people. She can communicate in four ways: crying, sounds, facial expressions, and gestures. She will be able to distinguish between a friendly and an angry voice, and will react differently to smiling and scolding.

What you can do to help

■ *Imitate all your baby's sounds with changes of pitch and loudness;*
■ *If your baby is a "listener", interest her in subtle sounds. Play soft music, crunch up tissue paper, ring small bells, and put a glass mobile near her bed;*
■ *Introduce all visitors to your child so that she gets used to strangers.*

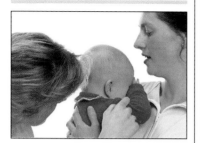

Catch her interest
If your baby listens rather than responds, make a variety of subtle noises that catch her attention.

24 WEEKS OLD

Your baby is making more overt and aggressive advances. He responds with gestures such as pats, strokes, scratches, and slaps. He may explore your face as a way of saying "Hello" or showing interest. At this time, he may show a fear of strangers, and will show possessiveness by hanging on and holding you.

What you can do to help

■ *If your baby makes lots of gestures, show him new ones. When you go to pick him up, stretch out your arms and he'll imitate you;*
■ *Make very big expansive gestures and pitch your voice to match your gesture. Wait for him to copy what you do;*
■ *Keep introducing strangers, and give your child plenty of time to adjust to them.*

Encourage new gestures
Respond to his gestures with variations so he'll learn a whole range of responses.

28 TO 36 WEEKS OLD

Your baby will look at, reach for, and touch another baby. He will want to join in games such as "Pat-A-Cake" and "This Little Piggy." In an attempt to be understood, your baby coughs, grunts, cries, shrieks, and makes raspberries and bubbles that join facial expressions and other conversational gestures.

What you can do to help

■ *Give a lot of physical affection. Encourage "touch" experiences and play lots of touch games;*
■ *If your baby babbles a lot, copy his voice variations. Then make a new sound, and wait for him to answer. He'll soon learn that sound means communication*
■ *Encourage independence through self-feeding; welcome experimentation;*
■ *Repeat the word "No" firmly so he understands the negative.*

Give lots of affection
Try to use every opportunity to touch your baby and to let him touch you.

SOCIABILITY

37 WEEKS TO ONE YEAR OLD

Your baby knows his own name and understands "No." He has a sense of humour and loves to make you laugh. He shows lots of affection by pressing his face and head against yours. He can remember some social rituals like "bye-bye" and kissing. If a toy is taken away he'll become angry.

What you can do to help
■ Use laughter to mean approval, and punctuate games and stories with laughs and jokes to develop his sense of humour in social exchanges;
■ Introduce him to other babies, and leave him occasionally with baby-sitters and others he doesn't know well. A baby will become dependent on one person if there is no other care-giver, and will become insecure on separation.

Demonstrate social rituals
When leaving, make certain to kiss and wave bye-bye; when arriving, give him a special greeting.

12 TO 15 MONTHS OLD

Your child enjoys social gatherings and will follow conversations, making noises in the gaps. He can say one or two words with meaning, ask for things, indicate thank you, and will refrain from doing things at the word "No." He tries to be helpful in activities. He likes to hold your hand for security.

What you can do to help
■ Place your baby so he can participate in social events. Put his highchair at the table, his playpen in the centre of the room, and his car seat between others;
■ Your child may show fear and dislike of strangers. Get him used to staying with others to foster independence;
■ Start to teach, "Thank you;"
■ Always take his hand and support him if he needs steadying.

Put him at the centre of things
Include your baby in as many activities as possible, and make certain he has a ring-side seat.

15 TO 18 MONTHS OLD

Your child is becoming more helpful, both with chores and dressing and undressing. She will show love to members of the family, pets, and dolls. She shows an increasing interest in adults, and wants to imitate them. She enjoys social gatherings. She plays next to, but not with, another child.

What you can do to help
■ Develop her helpful instincts by giving her simple chores;
■ Allow some dressing; she can put on her socks, and a hat;
■ Introduce her to other children as often as possible. She will be motivated to establish friendly relationships with others, due to the pleasure she derives from you. Encourage loving behaviour with relatives, other children, dolls, and family pets.

Encourage her to express love
Praise her when she shows affection and care towards others –siblings, relatives, pets, or toys.

18 MONTHS TO 2 YEARS OLD

Your child may indulge in attention-seeking devices such as grabbing your arm, hitting you, doing forbidden things, and often will refuse to obey. However, there is much less fighting and more cooperation with other children. She may modify selfish behaviour to accommodate a playmate.

What you can do to help
■ *Involve her with children as often as you can, have her play games with them, and provide all kinds of play materials to facilitate socializing;*
■ *Avoid rivalry by praising your child's achievements; this will give her a good sense of self-worth. Praise all sharing;*
■ *Always respond to attention-seeking devices but try to avoid negativism by using distracting tactics.*

Help her to understand sharing
Provide the means for interaction with others. Play group games and share out play materials.

2 TO 2½ YEARS OLD

Your child may find it hard to share well with others and will demonstrate feelings of rivalry. She will try to force her will on others. She wants to be independent but also seeks adult approval. She may react to authority with tantrums, which need to be ignored.

What you can do to help
■ *Always support her efforts. Overlook failure, and show how to sort out difficulties gently. Praise every success;*
■ *Start teaching manners and respect for private property. Be consistent about unbreakable rules like safety ones;*
■ *Use discipline sparingly but be fair and consistent with it; over-disciplining may lead to behavior problems, under-disciplining may lead to antisocial behaviour.*

Make sharing a game
Initiate games that involve giving others things, and she will learn to share with them.

3 YEARS OLD

Your child has become more independent from you and more outgoing towards other children. Unselfishness may start to blossom, and firm friendships with other adults and children may form. She will show signs of sympathy when someone is distressed and be more generous.

What you can do to help
■ *Unselfishness springs from being a team member so encourage your child to pull her own weight at home;*
■ *Give appreciation whenever possible;*
■ *It is never too early to introduce the necessity for truth and honesty. Always reward it even if it involves a confession to a misdemeanor. Reward the truth and deal with the misdemeanor next time. NEVER punish truth.*

Encourage play with others
Sharing leads to social acceptance, and this leads to generosity. Promote frequent contact with others.

BLADDER CONTROL

No two children gain bladder control at the same age. It is absolutely wrong to think that a child should be dry when you think it is time; the only time is when your child is ready, and by ready I mean when the brain, nerves, and muscles are sufficiently well-developed. The nerves are rarely mature and the muscles responsive to them until 15 to 18 months so please, for the sake of your child, don't expect great results from potty-sitting before then. Indeed, potty-sitting should never be enforced as this will simply make your child refuse to perform (and he always wins) and possibly lead to difficulties later, e.g. frequent accidents and/or bed-wetting.

Accidents are frequent in all children. What parents would do well to remember is that a child can barely hold urine for a second before 15 months old. So though he may alert you that he wants to pass urine, he can't hold it long enough for a potty to be fetched or to be sat on it. This is compounded by a natural increase in urinary frequency around 21 months, which no one can do anything about, least of all your baby. By 2½ years, your baby will be able to hold urine for up to four or five hours and thereafter, the holding span becomes longer.

From about 12 months old, babies go through a state of negativism so if your baby is forced to do anything against his will, he will simply refuse to comply. Determined and over-zealous attempts by parents to potty-train can result in total failure. All children love attention and fuss, and nothing pleases them more than to have the whole family carefully watching their efforts on the potty. A child loves mum sitting close cajoling, playing games, offering bribes, and finds that an accident immediately after removal of the potty throws the whole house into confusion, so he repeats the performance several times a day simply to get attention.

AVOIDING PROBLEMS WITH POTTY-TRAINING

☐ Problems are more likely to happen if you are determined to potty train your child early; the majority of disturbances with bladder control are due to forcing a child to stay on the potty and perform, and using discipline to enforce your wishes. Don't be overenthusiastic about potty training.

☐ Let your child develop at his own pace; there is no way that you can speed up the process – you are there to help him along. What you can do is to act quickly when your child signals that he has to pass urine, and to make certain a potty or toilet is readily available and easily accessible. Give plenty of praise, too.

☐ Help your child to stay dry at night by discouraging her having drinks within two hours of bedtime, making sure she empties her bladder before going to bed, and having her wear nightclothes that are easy to lift up or take down quickly.

☐ If you believe that your child is late in acquiring bladder control, specialist advice may be needed to rule out organic causes. Small bladder capacity, urethral obstruction or, in the case of a girl, an ectopic ureter all can result in incontinence.

BLADDER CONTROL

1 YEAR OLD

Your baby empties his bladder involuntarily, and has no control over it whatsoever. After meals is a common time for him to wet his nappy.

What you can do to help

■ *You can put your child on a potty for a few moments once he is able to sit up by himself, but don't expect to do more than catch any voided urine;*

■ *Don't stay overlong or encourage him, but if he does pass some urine, give him some mild praise;*

■ *Don't scold even if he wets just after getting off the potty.*

Make him familiar with the potty
Your baby won't be able to control his bladder for some time but you can get him ready by acquainting him with the potty.

13 MONTHS OLD

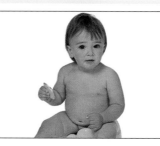

If placed on the potty after a meal your baby may use it successfully. However, she still is not able to control her bladder emptying.

What you can do to help

■ *Don't expect her to be able to control the voiding of urine. Take your lead from your child;*

■ *You can condition your child to sit on the potty after each meal for a few minutes, but this isn't the same as being trained.*

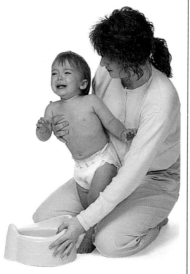

Conditioning can break down
The arrival of a sibling or other traumatic incident can interfere with whatever your baby has learned. Don't be concerned.

15 MONTHS OLD

Your child is now beginning to perceive when he feels the urge to void. However, he isn't very good at retaining urine, and will want to pass it very quickly.

What you can do to help

■ *Ask your child occasionally if he wants to go to the toilet. The answer "No" is pretty reliable;*

■ *Your baby won't be able to retain his urine for very long once he's attracted your attention, so just dismiss accidents cheerfully.*

Ask him if he wants the potty
When you think he might want to use the toilet, ask him to do so. Don't complain if he says "No" – it's the usual response.

18 MONTHS OLD

Your child's bladder and nerves are developed well enough now so that she can give you more warning but the system needs fine tuning still.

What you can do to help
■ Praise all successes and ignore failures completely;
■ Don't expect your child to stay dry through the night as the bladder capacity is not great enough yet.

Praise all successes
Every time your child uses the potty successfully make sure she knows what a good thing you think it is, and that you are pleased.

21 MONTHS OLD

Around this time your toddler may be going through a phase of increased frequency. This is natural and so is the increased frequency of accidents.

What you can do to help
■ Be philosophical. Don't increase potty-sitting time.

Ignore failures completely
It is natural for your child to make mistakes at this early age. When accidents do happen, simply change your child without making a fuss.

2 YEARS OLD

Your baby is very proud of her ability to manage going to the potty herself. She may demand to be left alone when she goes to the potty.

What you can do to help
■ If you want her to use a toilet, make certain she can reach it easily, that the seat is not too big for her, and that the room is always well lit;
■ Give your baby all the freedom and support she requires. Let her make her own mistakes; this will encourage her independence and pride and will speed up her bladder control.

Help her to be independent
Make certain she can reach the toilet without help and that the seat fits her snugly. Be close by in case she needs your help.

BLADDER CONTROL

2 ½ YEARS OLD

Your baby is so sure of herself that she asks not to wear a nappy during the day and is able to stay dry most of the time.

What you can do to help
■ *Provide thick "training" pants instead of a nappy if she asks;*
■ *Don't expect her to be dry at night, or not to have frequent accidents.*

Provide "training" pants
Special thicker pants are available that provide a bit more protection in case of accidents than regular ones do. Encourage your child to use them.

3 YEARS OLD

Your child may stay dry through the night if taken to the toilet before you go to bed. Normally this does not disturb her rest.

What you can do to help
■ *Take her to the toilet before you go to bed;*
■ *If she stays dry for three consecutive nights, try leaving off her night-time nappy;*
■ *Place a potty at her bedside for your child to use when she feels the need.*

To help her stay dry
Place a potty near her bed so she can use it if she wakes in the night. Continue to protect her bed with a rubber sheet for some time.

TRAINING TIPS
■ *Girls usually have control over their bladders and bowels earlier than boys. Most babies will stay dry sooner or later than the average age given;*
■ *By 18 months most children are almost dry during the day; by 2 years half will be dry at night; by 3 years three-quarters are dry day and night; by 5 years 90% are dry day and night. So it follows that 1 out of 10 children still will be wetting the bed at 5; this is normal;*
■ *The development of bladder control can't be accelerated but it can be slowed up – especially by you. The commonest cause of slow sphincter control is an obsessive or authoritarian parent. The second is one who doesn't care at all;*
■ *You couldn't be more wrong if you think your child is refusing the potty out of naughtiness. He is not; your behaviour has trained him to behave that way. So please don't punish and NEVER smack him;*
■ *Small bladder capacity (can't wait long enough) may be a cause of frequent accidents and is often inherited; so the chances are that one of you handed it down to your child. You can't blame a child for something he has inherited;*
■ *If your child is dry and then starts to wet again, a high level of anxiety is commonly at the root of your child's problem. The commonest causes of anxiety in children are separation from parents, parental strife, and tension in the family.*

BOWEL CONTROL

Bowel control usually happens before bladder control but there is a greater variation in the time when bowel control is achieved. Some babies seem to move smoothly from passing a stool reflexively after a meal to voluntary stool voiding, which is totally under their control. Others (particularly boys), on the other hand, may show no sign of control until after two. That is how wide the spread of normality is. There is also a wide range, 12 months to 2 ½ years, during which children may play with the stool and smear it. This is because children are fascinated with what comes out of their bodies, not because they have dirty habits, so please remember this and distract them, never scold them for something that is so natural.

Just as children love being the centre of attention by manipulating their parents over bladder control, they quickly learn, if you show your obsessiveness, to use the whole process of bowel control, potty-sitting, passing stools, as something with which they can claim all your attention and regard. Your child is quick to learn that Mummy and Daddy will make a fuss of her if she DOESN'T pass a stool so you can encourage constipation in your child with inappropriate behaviour. And remember, you can't win, ever. The more fuss you make, the more delighted your child is because the more control she holds over you.

So just as with bladder control, your role is to let your child develop at her own pace and to make it easy for her to do so. Don't be overenthusiastic about potty training but be full of praise when your child stays clean. And should she have an accident, don't make a fuss over it.

BOWEL CONTROL

15 TO 18 MONTHS OLD

Your baby empties her bowel after eating because of the gastro-colic reflex. She is not yet ready to use the potty, but you may be able to catch stools after meals.

What you can do to help
■ *It is too soon for your baby to begin potty training, but you can condition her to get used to sitting on a potty;*
■ *As soon as your baby can sit up on her own, put her on the potty only after meals;*
■ *Never leave her longer than a few moments, and if she gets bored, let her get off;*
■ *Say "Well done" if she passes a stool, and don't comment if she doesn't.*

Get her used to the potty
After a meal, when she is able to sit up by herself, put her on the potty for as long as she wants to stay, but no more than a few minutes.

18 MONTHS TO 2 YEARS OLD

Your child is happy and relaxed sitting on, or playing with, the potty.

What you can do to help
■ *Always let him come into the toilet with you, so he can imitate you when he is ready;*
■ *Encourage him to feel happy and relaxed whatever he does with, or in, the potty.*

Let him join you in the toilet
Don't discourage your child from coming into the toilet with you. He will imitate your actions when he's ready to relieve himself voluntarily.

2 TO 2½ YEARS OLD

Your child's desire to be clean and independent is very keen, but take the lead in training only from her wishes.

What you can do to help
■ *Encourage your child by praising her after a clean night, even though she still may be wet;*
■ *Don't be too anxious about wanting her to stay clean. Wait for her to signal or request.*

Give praise if she stays clean
Bowel training is accomplished before bladder training, so it is important to discriminate between the two and praise each achievement as it occurs.

2 ½ TO 5 YEARS OLD

Your child can now control and retain her stool so that she has time to get to the toilet without an accident.

What you can do to help
■ Most children are clean by 5, but by no means all. Stay calm;
■ Dress her in clothes that are easy for her to remove when she has to use the toilet.

Don't force; don't fuss
Most children will have occasional accidents even after they have been clean for some time. Should an accident occur, don't make a fuss over it.

TRAINING TIPS

■ *Breast-fed babies pass stools infrequently; this is normal; it is not constipation; do not worry about it;*
■ *Most parents, but particularly mothers, consider that a daily motion is essential, whereas it is not.*
■ *The parent, whose child withholds stools, is often one who examines the potty after every movement to see if it is enough;*
■ *If you ever find yourself holding down a kicking, screaming child on the potty, desist; bowel problems will surely follow;*
■ *Constipation is common in children whose mothers make them sit on the potty when they don't want to;*
■ *If your baby has gained bowel control then loses it, psychological upset is the commonest cause; look to yourself and your family first for the reasons;*
■ *Chronic constipation in a child, paradoxically, may appear as diarrhoea, as the bowel secretes extra fluid to move the stool along;*
■ *Soiling seems to be associated with a high rate of parental divorce and separation;*
■ *Soiling appears to have an association with "problem parents" — a passive father and a domineering mother;*
■ *Persistent soiling may be a condition, predominantly of boys, who have been forcibly toilet trained;*
■ *The golden rule is no forcing, no fussing.*

PERSONALITY

To be happy, our children have to make good personal as well as social adjustments. In a culture such as ours where social life is very complex, personality is important.

It is important for parents to understand that their child's personality is more dependent on what their child learns from them than anything that is inherited. The "chip off the old block" theory is long outdated. This means that parents must shoulder responsibility for how their children turn out, and therefore take care over developing traits in their children that will serve them well in later life.

Many features of your child's personality will affect his future prospects such as the ability to relate to people and rub along; to learn from mistakes; the willingness to muck in and work hard; the power to observe, concentrate, enquire; the ability to be creative, thorough, determined, ambitious. All these will help a child, while characteristics such as laziness, inability to concentrate, slow thinking, inability to express him or herself, will hold your child back. Parents can affect profoundly the acquisition of these personality features, and can do much to strengthen inborn traits such as independence, responsiveness (a "ready" smile), thoroughness, a placid nature, self-reliance.

Parents also must take responsibility for wittingly or unwittingly imposing their own character traits on their children: an impatient parent rarely has a patient child; a difficult child often has a difficult parent. A "difficult" child often is responding normally to a difficult family set-up. A placid parent who takes everything in her stride is very unlikely to have a difficult child. Remember your child's whole life is moulded in the first few years, even months. If your child's basic needs are met, and he receives lots of love, attention, and stimulation, then it is likely that he will grow up a happy person.

NEWBORN TO 36 WEEKS OLD

Your baby will exhibit an independent personality from the moment he is born. You discern this from his basic activities. He may cry rarely, even when tired, and is placid and happy. Or, he may demand attention, let you know the moment he is hungry, tired, and bored by crying, and be active and determined.

When feeding, your baby may take the breast or bottle easily, suck well and be satisfied. Or, he may have difficulty latching on, sucks for a minute only, fusses, cries, screams, and upsets you. He may tolerate hunger well, appear patient and lie still while feeding; or, he may be impatient, and throw up a lot after feeding.

He may sleep most of the day and rarely get ruffled. On the other hand, he may be awake for hours, discard his midday nap very young, and require company and games, and refuse to be left alone even at a few weeks of age.

Your baby may be social — loving company, cuddles, toys and people. Or he may not. He may appear to reject most things.

What you can do to help

■ Trust, warmth and outgoingness are developed in the first few months, and at this time you must teach your baby most of the basic ways to relate to people. So most importantly, be POSITIVE in all you do, and OVERT in all you express;

■ Smiling is your most important tool to show pleasure, approval, love, and joy. Voice comes next. Babies are sensitive to loving, approving, delighted and joyful tones of voice, pitched light and high. They will also respond to comforting, soothing, and quietening tones. Avoid sharp, negative ones;

■ Body contact – the warmth, closeness and smell of your body is important, too, as are touches and physical demonstrations of affection;

■ Encourage endlessly, reward often, praise constantly, give approval unstintingly, and always use your baby's name in a loving context. Say "I love you" as often as possible. Reinforce all good traits with praise and encouragement;

■ Always answer requests for attention; otherwise your child will regard himself as unimportant and will stop asking you. Make eye contact with him, face him, use gestures and touch to communicate feelings of worth;

■ Don't be negative; use distraction techniques to overcome any negativism on your baby's part.

36 WEEKS TO 18 MONTHS OLD

Your baby has become more distinctly herself, showing that she is serious, sensitive, independent, sociable, irritable, perverse, determined, able to concentrate, curious, impatient, etc. Once she is a year old, your baby will show how determined and independent she is by going through a stage of negativism, becoming impatient, difficult, short-tempered, irritable, defiant, naughty, and unloving.

By 15 months, however, a new thoughtful, helpful stage will emerge, and she will show an obvious desire to please. She will strive for your approval and be desolated when you disapprove of her.

What you can do to help

■ Be flexible in everything, and never use force. Don't criticize, don't be hostile. Never make your child fear you. Teach patience through tolerance, never ridicule, don't make your child feel ashamed, don't let her feel jealous, or she will learn to feel guilty;

■ Accept her as she is, and she will learn to love. If you praise her, she'll be appreciative; if you express approval she will like herself. If you recognize her efforts, she will set her own goals; if you are fair, she will value justice; if you are truthful, she will learn to be honest; if you give security, she will have faith in herself and others.

PERSONALITY

18 MONTHS TO 2 YEARS OLD

Your toddler may want to help others and do everything for herself, or, she may want everything done for her. She may be incautious or careful, imaginative or with feet on the ground, take criticism easily, or be reduced to tears. She may be a born leader or follower.

What you can do to help

■ Show your toddler how to tackle problems; accept her decisions easily, without worry or conflict. Gradually increase her responsibilities. Give your toddler the time to concentrate on important things so she can complete a task, but always help if asked. Diffuse frustration with distraction;

■ Make time for games. Spend special time together and always show sympathy for difficulties or pain;

■ Encourage your toddler to be generous; she will want to please you, so take advantage of this by teaching generous acts, like giving you a plate of her ice-cream, and then go on to encourage more of the same towards other members of the family;

■ If yours is an only child, you must curb her desire to have all that she wants, and all your attention. A child should learn she cannot be the permanent centre of your world.

2 TO 3 YEARS OLD

Your child's personality has emerged clearly. She is an individual person and family member, with an expanding sense of self. Everything she does is a test for her to measure achievement, capability and ability; she defines herself through what she can do, and how successfully she does it, in terms of physical performance, communication, manual dexterity, thinking, and skill. Success is crucial to her in mastering skills, daily routines, and managing on her own.

What you can do to help

■ Success is the greatest positive influence in personality development, so help your child to succeed, and make sure she is often successful at doing things, because it will encourage a sense of pride and satisfaction;

■ Help your child to seek new challenges. Those that will make her independent and self-reliant, daring, unselfconcious, prepared to take responsibility and blame, should be encouraged;

■ Raise her aspirations and build up her self-confidence and self-image without sacrificing cheerfulness and happiness. Teach her to say "Sorry," and respect the rights of others;

■ Lessen any fears your child may have by reassuring her that you will return when you go out. Listen to and observe your toddler, as closely as possible, to pick up clues as to what might be bothering her. Talk over any fears, and reassure her. All fears have to be handled sympathetically, and quickly. Never ridicule fear. Explanations and sympathy are what's needed.

SPEECH

The basics of language are built into most babies' brains. A deaf infant starts to babble at the same age as does a hearing child, so we know that auditory stimulation is not necessary for language development. Some theorists even say we have a "language acquisition device" somewhere in the brain that makes language inevitable. Language and speech are closely intertwined; we can define language as the general term for verbal symbols and speech as its means of expression; both reflect an instinctive human need to communicate. This need is obvious in very young babies as they bob and mouthe in response to verbal overtures. By six weeks, a baby who is talked to often can be in control of a "conversation" because already she has learned that sounds, gestures, and body language unfailingly elicit responses from the person with whom she is conversing.

We underestimate an infant's desire and ability to imitate; if talked to often, a baby will start to imitate sounds as early as eight weeks, and has already taken the first major step towards speech acquisition. This means that parents must surround their children with speech using talk, songs, rhymes, running commentary, specific conversations. Stressing words, using rhythm, and repeating simple sounds help a baby's brain to make those millions of neural connections required for full speech development.

We also know that language throughout life is closely linked to emotion, and children who get unconditional love and lots of cuddling have a better chance of learning language than those who do not receive overt affection. Conversation is a game; babies love to play it. Show your baby the rules from day one and both your lives will be inestimably the better for it.

SPEECH

NEWBORN TO 8 WEEKS OLD

In the early stages of learning to speak, your baby will listen and try to imitate sounds. She will respond to high-pitched human sounds from the moment of birth. She will observe and try to imitate gestures and expressions. Her eyes may flick towards a sound, and her gaze will become intent. She will watch a talking face placed eight to ten inches away from hers. Your baby will sense two-way communication, and try to converse with sounds, gestures, and body language. She will make sounds to initiate intercourse, to elicit a response, and also to respond to overtures. From two weeks of age, she will engage in "conversation." By six weeks your baby will recognize your voice, and at eight weeks, she will respond to it.

What you can do to help

■ The more your baby is stimulated to talk by being talked to and encouraged to respond, the earlier she will learn to talk, and the better will be the quality of her speech. So talk non-stop from day one, and be very theatrical with all of your conversations;

■ Reward communication with smiles, cuddles, and attention, and you will increase your baby's motivation to speak;

■ Show lots of physical affection, and affection in your vocal tones, which will forge close emotional links between you and your baby, and provide her with lots of encouragement;

■ Eye contact is crucial for your baby to understand your interest, love, concern, and attention. Make a point of achieving eye contact all the time. Take the trouble to turn your body towards your baby and face her;

■ Learn her basic vocabulary of crying. Always answer a request made that way, whether it's about hunger, tiredness, boredom, or affection, and never leave your baby to cry.

8 TO 24 WEEKS OLD

One to two weeks after smiling at you, your baby may begin to vocalize with simple vowel sounds such as "eh," "ah," "uh," "oh." About a month later consonants may be added, usually "m," "p," and "b" when displeased, and "j" and "k" when happy. At 12 weeks your baby squeals with pleasure, and in the next few weeks your baby will attempt to "hold a conversation," with imitation sentences made up of sounds like "gaga," "ah goo," "ug." By 16 weeks, he has a language of sounds comprising laughing or loud squeals of delight, blowing between his lips, and blowing bubbles. Towards 24 weeks, your baby adds "ka," "da," "ma," and "ergh" to his vocabulary.

There are many signs that your baby is beginning to understand what you say. He begins to babble — playing with sounds by repeating them and listening to them.

What you can do to help

■ To speak a child has to learn the mechanics of speech, through movements of the tongue, lips, and palate, so sucking, licking, blowing bubbles, and chewing are all important skills to acquire and practise. Encourage them with games, and eventually through feeding;

■ Children who are sung to, have nursery rhymes repeated to them, have rhythms in speech emphasized, and are involved in singing and rhyming games, speak more easily and better than children who don't. So engage in all these things from a very early age;

■ One of the first ways babies communicate is through laughter. Make talking amusing, funny, humorous. Laugh and giggle a lot;

■ In the early months, babies learn from imitation so it's crucial to repeat names, routines, and events. Intone dramatically and use actions whenever possible. If you say "hot!", say it breathily; add "ouch" and withdraw your hand suddenly, and jump about as though in pain; repeat "hot."

28 WEEKS TO ONE YEAR OLD

At 28 weeks clear syllables emerge — "ba!", "da ", "ka!". Your baby's cries have a variety of high- and low- pitched sounds and a nasal sound appears. She has started to play games with her tongue and lips, and may use sound to attract your attention — a squeal or a cough. At 32 weeks syllables are combined clearly "ba-ba" and "da-da."

She will then gradually add the sounds of "t," "d," and "w" and then, at around 36 to 40 weeks, she will imitate real speech sounds. At 40 weeks she may use one word with meaning, by 48 weeks she will almost certainly do so.

Understanding, an essential forerunner to speech, has been increasing rapidly and at 40 weeks, most babies understand "No." Your baby also may obey several simple orders, as in acting out nursery rhymes, playing "Pat-A-Cake" and waving bye-bye. She may imitate animal sounds, "moo," "quack," "miaow," and "woof."

What you can do to help

■ If your child is going to learn to pronounce words correctly, and later combine them into correct sentences, you must be a model of good speech for her to imitate. So speak clearly, slowly, and embellish meaning with actions, expressions, and gestures;

■ To help your child to speak you are going to have to lose some of your inhibitions, and start babbling with her. She'll look at you and giggle, and try again even harder. You reiterate your babble, so learning to speak becomes a game for both of you;

■ Babble when your baby babbles, but speak a lot normally, too. As soon as your child says one possible word, repeat it. Show your pleasure. Say what a clever girl she is. Repeat "ma" and laugh and give her a hug. She'll say "ma" over and over, delighted at her own cleverness;

■ Children can speak only when words have meaning. They must understand the meaning of a word long before they can say it. Demonstrate meaning over and over again with pictures, gestures, actions, etc.

1 YEAR TO 18 MONTHS OLD

Your toddler may say two or three words with meaning, but even before saying them, he recognizes a few simple objects when pointed out. Some of his words are acquired back-wards e.g. he may start saying "g" for dog, then "og," and finally "dog." Others may start from the front, e.g. "g" for girl. At about 15 months, he may break gradually into jargon, which is strings of his own unintelligible sounds, but with emphases, inflections, phrasing, actions, and the odd real word. These are practice runs at stringing real words togethim. He may repeat a short phrase, which you say often, e.g. "Dear me," in appropriate circumstances. At 18 months old, your toddler may be able to point out many objects in books and everyday life. He should be able to use about 10 words with meaning.

What you can do to help

Having become more mobile, your toddler's comprehension is miles ahead of his ability to express himself, e.g. "Mama" can mean lots of things, including "Mummy, give me a drink." When you discover what she means, say "Mummy will get you a drink," and say the word drink again. Soon he'll say, "Mummy, dink;"

■ Introduce your toddler to all kinds of noises, such as those made by animals, vehicles, and music. He is very switched on to sounds, so point them out: doors squeak, taps drip, paper rustles;

■ Read books as often as you can, going over and over favourite ones, repeating names and objects. Point to familiar objects. Give their names. Ask him to repeat the names. Show pleasure when he remembers;

■ Name everything, everywhere. Name colours, textures, other properties;

■ Start counting and use numbers whenever the opportunity arises.

SPEECH

18 MONTHS TO 2 YEARS OLD

Your toddler's speech now becomes more complex and sophisticated. He may have a vocabulary of 30 words. and starts to ask simple questions, such as "Where gone?" and gives one- or two- word answers, "There." In fact, he uses many two-word combinations. Added to his vocabulary are possessives, "mine," and negatives, "can't."

The rhythm of conversing is being learned, and your toddler waits and takes his turn at speaking. He is becoming cooperative in communicating. He uses language in different situations — to get something, to tell about something, to relate to others. His speech, however, may be indistinct because of poor muscle coordination. He may say "tebbair" instead of "teddy bear."

What you can do to help

■ Start to use adjectives whenever you can. The first are usually "good," "bad," "nice," "nasty," "hot," "cold." Couple them with nouns, "cold milk," "nice girl," "good teddy," especially when you are describing food, people and toys — your toddler's favourite subjects;

■ Use adverbs, too, such as "here" and "where." Emphasize all verbs, and add actions to promote understanding;

■ Prepositions are understood long before your toddler uses them, but always stress them and show what you mean. Always indicate where "under", "on top of," and "behind" are;

■ Language acquisition is not smooth, it stops and starts, so follow your toddler's lead and don't press. Don't compare your child with anyone else; language is learned at different rates by different children.

2 TO 3 YEARS OLD

Your child knows about 200 to 300 words, and she may engage in long monologues. She uses language confidently, and shows interest in new words. She is beginning to listen when reasoned with, and her span of interest is getting wider and longer. Fluency in speech is improving, even though words are mispronounced, letters may be substituted incorrectly, and lisping is common.

Your child starts to develop language rituals such as hearing the same story over and over. She likes complicated stories, and to listen to adult conversation. She can jump from one topic to another in a single sentence.

Your child is starting to use the word "and" to connect ideas. She also is getting the hang of pronouns such as "I," "me," "you," and uses them correctly. Lots of words to do with time are appearing as she understands the concepts of past, present, and future.

What you can do to help

■ Your child will talk more to children of her own age than to adults, so exposing her as often as possible to the company of other children will help develop her linguistic abilities. This is one of the reasons why nursery school becomes important. At this age, speech ceases to be egocentric and becomes more social, so contact with other children is essential if your child is to develop social language;

■ Repeat favourite stories, so that your child can work out her feelings about the world about her;

■ Read more complex stories, and introduce new words, explaining them by using them over and over in your speech.

3 TO 4 YEARS OLD

Your child is showing command of language and confidence in using it; consequently she is becoming more fluent and daring. She loves new words, and practises using them. She realises that she can exert some degree of control with language, so starts to use words like commands ("Bring me"), persuasion ("Please may I have"), cooperation ("I'll try"). Your child is starting to use interesting tenses of verbs like the conditional ("I wish I could have an ice cream."), and understands the concept of possibility and probability ("I might go to Granny's."; "Perhaps it will rain."; "Maybe we'll get an ice-cream."). The concept of grammar is growing fast, e.g. if something happened in the past she puts "ed" on the end of the word ("He hitted me."), and gets plurals slightly wrong ("mouses") but has a try at comparatives ("badder," "gooder"). She likes to keep a conversation going with questions "how?", "why?", "when?", uses slang, nonsense words, and may make up her own words.

What you can do to help

■ Never overtly correct your child's mistakes; diplomatically repeat what she has just said, but correctly. If she hesitates over a word, supply it instantly, to maintain her momentum and interest;

■ Your child responds well to reasoning, so include her in simple problem solving, with questions, options, solutions — openly discussing each step. Ask her opinion about something you know you can agree with, so that she feels she has made the decisions;

■ Make sentences longer and more complex. When your child speaks to you, turn to her and listen attentively. Nod, and incline your head to show you are listening;

■ Always answer questions. There is no need to tell the whole truth, just the amount that she can handle, but never lie or dissemble. Your child will find you out and mistrust you. Your child will ask the same question over and over; just give the same answer, never become impatient;

■ Children like whispering so play whispering games to aid expression;

■ In your child's list of reading include fairy stories, because they help your child to come to terms with her own world without it hurting her, and because they improve her concepts of real and unreal; past, present and future; fairness and injustice; good and evil; kindness and brutality, and so on.

FACTORS AFFECTING DEVELOP- MENT

FACTORS AFFECTING DEVELOPMENT

Though at times your child's development may seem haphazard and disjointed, the goal is always the same – to achieve genetic potential or full self-realisation. Each and every child is born with the desire to strive to be the best person possible; both physically and mentally your child has the urge to do what she is best fitted to do, to be happy and well adjusted. To be so, your child must be given the opportunity to fulfil this urge.

Whether your child will achieve this goal depends on what obstacles she encounters, and how successful she is in overcoming them. The obstacles may be in your child's environment, or they may be from within your child herself; for example, she may be fearful of attempting to do what she is capable of doing, perhaps because of criticism or comparison with others.

Your role is crucial in helping your child reach his or her potential. You must not only be aware of the many different factors that have an effect on it but you must act appropriately to maximize or minimize their influences. If you follow the guidelines set out below, you will find these "jobs" a lot easier.

HEALTH

Among the several things that aid your child to reach self-realisation, health is the main-stay because it helps a child to attack problems more vigorously than he could if his health was undermined. It follows, therefore, that freedom from serious physical defects, which handicap a child in whatever he attempts to do, is an advantage.

Most of us take the good health of our children for granted, but it plays an immeasurably important role in their development. This can be seen if we look at the common effects of ill-health. While ordinary childhood diseases seldom have a permanent effect upon growth and development, a long and severe illness may stunt this process if it coincides with a period of rapid development.

During illness, most children are inactive and muscles may lose some of their tone becoming easily fatigued, so a child's development may be temporarily halted.

Illness nearly always makes a child irritable, and he is more likely to be anxious and have temper tantrums. Illness and recuperation often require restriction of activities, and a child finds this very frustrating – sometimes becoming unsure of himself as an individual but also in relation to other children.

An illness may often be the starting point for adjustment problems such as finicky eating and other behavioural difficulties. This is particularly so if a child is pampered, in which case he may develop unhealthy attitudes about his own importance. A child may become so accustomed to special attention that he is aggressive and demanding after he recovers. If this behaviour persists, it is certain that it will affect his development in all areas but particularly in his relationships with others.

Chronic diseases such as epilepsy and diabetes, in particular, can hamper a child, mainly because they may cause emotional instability and occasionally strong negative emotions, if not handled carefully. They can affect a child's development because they produce emotional dependence on other family members.

Certain common physical conditions such as fatigue and over-tiredness can cause your child to be irritable and quarrelsome, which will always affect his reactions to people and theirs to him. Malnutrition and a lack of a balanced diet can lead to a low energy level, which not only curtails physical activities and qualities such as curiosity and adventurousness, but also strength, stamina and, therefore, enjoyment and learning. They may also produce shyness, irritability, depression, and anti-social behaviour. A minor physical complaint such as eczema or another form of skin rash can produce physical irritation, and this can lead to emotional over-reactions, the inability to concentrate, and the lack of determination to follow a project through or complete a task.

HAPPINESS

Happy children are normally healthy and energetic, and happiness of itself supplies a strong motivation to do things. On the whole, happy children accept frustrations and obstacles more calmly and try to find ways around them. Happiness, of course, encourages all kinds of social contacts and social activities – people usually react positively to cheerfulness, and happiness gives a child a friendly expression, a good starting point for all kinds of personal relationships.

Unhappiness, on the other hand, saps a child's strength and energy, and lowers her general physical well-being. This, in turn, prevents her energy from being directed into purposeful activities, so quite often unhappy children dissipate their energies in brooding, daydreaming, and self-pity, and the unhappy child tends to be withdrawn and self-regarding. Unhappiness stifles motivation, determination, and the desire to succeed. Temper tantrums and obstructive behaviour are much more common in unhappy children and prevent them learning from experience.

Happiness can become a habit, and it is your job to make sure that your child acquires this habit. Similarly unhappiness can develop into a habit, and it is your job to prevent it. Of course, a happy childhood is no guarantee of adult success but the one thing that it does do is to lay the foundation for success, while unhappiness lays only the foundation for failure.

PARENTAL ATTITUDES

Your general attitude towards parenthood will greatly affect your child's experiences as he grows up and will influence his development. Now that you have a child, the best possible start you can give him is a positive attitude to being his parent.

Some people want many children, others want a few or none. Many people still feel that a marriage is incomplete without children and others feel that children are an obstacle to career success and upward mobility. If you belong to the latter group it will be very difficult to score highly on the criteria for the ideal parent. If you aspire to being a good parent, the list below, of childrens' concepts of good parents, may be of help.

Older parents, in general, welcome their parental roles more wholeheartedly than younger ones, and parenthood is helped if parents do not have the romanticized picture of children and

A GOOD PARENT

- ☐ *Does things for his/her child*
- ☐ *Can be depended on by his/her child*
- ☐ *Is reasonably permissive and giving*
- ☐ *Is fair in discipline*
- ☐ *Respects his/her child's individuality*
- ☐ *Inspires love not fear*
- ☐ *Sets a good example*
- ☐ *Is companionable and does things with his/her child*
- ☐ *Is good natured most of the time*
- ☐ *Shows his/her child affection*
- ☐ *Is sympathetic when his/her child is hurt or in trouble*

- ☐ *Encourages his/her child to bring friends to the home*
- ☐ *Is interested in making a happy home*
- ☐ *Grants independence appropriate for his/her child's age*
- ☐ *Does not expect unreasonable achievements*

parenthood that is often portrayed in the mass media. It is unrealistic to expect any child to live up to this, and having a highly idealized concept of your child, a "dream" child for instance, can be really dangerous and can only lead to disappointment and resentment when he does not conform to your expectations.

How you can help your child

The child who has the most confidence is one who accepts himself, and this favourable concept of himself largely depends on your attitude to him. This kind of child can cope with any problem that life throws at him.

One of the most important things you can do for your child is to keep him in the real world and to set realistic goals so that failures are avoided and his self concept is left undamaged. On the other hand, it is up to you to point out to your child weaknesses as well as strengths, though always concentrating on the latter, so he grows up with an understanding of himself and a knowledge of his limitations.

Make sure that the environment you create around your child does not limit his opportunities for learning because, if opportunities are limited, he will be unable to reach his full potential.

Don't try to fit your child into a set pattern; this is one of the most discouraging environments for him to live in. What a child requires is the encouragement to develop his own individuality. By helping him to meet and cope with problems that are too difficult for him to meet alone, you will teach self-assurance and determination.

Bear in mind, too, for full development, your child's innate capabilities must be stimulated and encouraged at the time when he is ready. Timing is, therefore, of the essence. Regardless of how much effort a child puts into learning, he cannot learn until he is developmentally ready. But once he is ready, the speed of development will be astonishing, especially if you boost his interests and efforts with encouragement.

Often you will notice that your child reaches a temporary plateau in his development and it is easy for you to conclude that he has reached his limit. As a result, your child will make little effort to learn more and will remain on the plateau whereas, with a little encouragement from you, he could advance to even higher levels, once you see that further attainment is always possible.

One other important responsibility as a parent is to teach your child to relate to and be aware of others, to be orientated to people other than herself. This will ensure that she will find it easy to make friends and avoid the solitary life of a loner. Your child will never be socially accepted if unsocial behaviour goes unchallenged. It is important that it is corrected before it becomes habitual and jeopardizes her chances of being one of the gang.

YOUR CHILD'S POSITION IN THE FAMILY

No position in the family can be regarded as best. First-born children grow in a more child-centered environment where the family activities concentrate on the child more than around later born children. First-born children have more guidance and help in their development, receive more complex language from their parents during infancy, and because of parental pressures on them, they usually achieve more than latter-born siblings. First-born children tend to be better accepted by grown-ups and are more likely to take up leadership roles because they conform more closely to social expectations. On the other hand, parents are less skilled at parenting with the first child and tend to intervene, intrude, restrict and use more coercive discipline and more punishments of all kinds than they do with later children. This can lead to first children receiving more feelings of anxiety from their parents, in other words "Am I doing right?". However, there is little doubt that if children born later in the family were given the same guidance and attention as first borns, they probably would achieve as much and be as well accepted socially.

The effects of family position become persistent very quickly and greatly influence the personal and social adjustments children make as they grow up. For instance, there is evidence that first borns are more health conscious than their younger siblings and as adults consult doctors more often. They also tend to be more cautious and take fewer risks.

Family position has been found to have an important influence on the way adults make marital adjustments. This is because we all learn to play certain roles in our childhood homes and continue to play those roles after marriage. For instance, the best marital adjustments have been where husbands who are the oldest brothers marry younger sisters. There is likely to be friction when these positions are reversed because wives try to boss their husbands as they did their younger brothers. In a marriage where husband and wife are both first borns, there is likely to be a highly frictional relationship with each trying to dominate the other.

The number of children in a family

The number of small children in the family greatly affects a child's development. Children with several young brothers and sisters must share parental attention. If one child is weaker, he is likely to get the lion's share of parental attention leading to sensitivity about favouritism in the others. Rivalry between siblings, competition, bad feelings, and resentment will be heightened. In addition, a weaker child is likely to develop a follower personality pattern, and feelings of inadequacy and martyrdom, while the stronger may feel discriminated against and learns to play the leader.

PERSONALITY CHARACTERISTICS ATTRIBUTED TO BIRTH ORDER

FIRST BORN

- ☐ *Uncertainty*
- ☐ *Mistrustfulness*
- ☐ *Insecurity*
- ☐ *Shrewdness*
- ☐ *Stinginess*
- ☐ *Dependency*
- ☐ *Responsibility*
- ☐ *Authoritarianism*
- ☐ *Jealousy*
- ☐ *Conservatism*
- ☐ *Suggestibility*
- ☐ *Excitability*

- ☐ *Sensitiveness*
- ☐ *Self-achievement drive*
- ☐ *Need for affiliation*

THIRD BORN

- ☐ *Aggressiveness*
- ☐ *Distractability*
- ☐ *A craving for demonstrations of affection*
- ☐ *Jealousy*
- ☐ *Being plagued by feelings of parental neglect*
- ☐ *Inferiority*
- ☐ *Inadequacy*
- ☐ *Proneness to behaviour disorders*

SECOND BORN

- ☐ *Independence*
- ☐ *Aggressiveness*
- ☐ *Extroversion*
- ☐ *Funlovingness*
- ☐ *Gregariousness*
- ☐ *Dependability*
- ☐ *A placid and even temperament*

LAST BORN

- ☐ *Security*
- ☐ *Confidence*
- ☐ *Spontaneity*
- ☐ *Good-naturedness*
- ☐ *Generosity*
- ☐ *Being spoiled*
- ☐ *Immaturity*
- ☐ *Extroversion*
- ☐ *An ability to empathise*
- ☐ *Feelings of inadequacy*
- ☐ *Inferiority*
- ☐ *Sibling rivalry*

- ☐ *Envy and jealousy*
- ☐ *Irresponsibility*
- ☐ *Happiness*

There is less space and fewer resources all around in a crowded family. Children are thrown together constantly and are expected to play together, share the same toys and friends, and dress alike even when they are not of the same sex. This obviously stifles the development of personality and individuality. The spacing of children is crucial. Where possible, the optimum time for a child to have with her parents before a new sibling comes along is 2 to 2½ years.

GENDER

There are two main effects of gender: the first is a direct effect of sex on development and comes from the very small quantity of hormones that boys and girls secrete throughout the childhood years. Both sexes produce androgen, the male hormone, and oestrogen, the female hormone, but boys produce more androgen and girls more oestrogen and it is the predominance of the appropriate sex hormone that is responsible for the differences in their development.

The indirect effect of sex on development comes from environmental conditions. From the time children are born, strong social pressures are put on them to conform to the culturally approved patterns for their sexes. Throughout the childhood years, both boys and girls are moulded first by family, later by peer and school groups, and still later by teachers and society into a pattern that is considered appropriate for the child's sex.

Sex differences in skill aquisition While children of the same sex differ more from each other than do girls from boys, the vast majority of parents would recognize that gender differences affect not only the rate of development of certain skills but also their type. In the area of physical development, for instance, girls appear to be on a faster timetable all the way through their growth, and mature at adolescence earlier than boys. In addition, a girl's physical growth is more regular and predictable than boys, with fewer uneven spurts. As far as strength and speed are concerned, there is little difference between boys and girls until puberty, when boys become both stronger and faster, and have more muscle, more bone and less fat. As would be expected, at puberty boys develop larger hearts and lungs to cope with the greater oxygen-carrying capacity needed by the blood for their larger muscle and bone masses.

In the pre-school years, girls are better at jumping, hopping, and rhythmic movement and balance. Later, boys are better at activities requiring running, jumping, and throwing, while girls remain better at hopping. In terms of intellectual development, there is no difference between boys and girls when I.Q. Tests are performed. However, as far as verbal skills are concerned, girls are slightly faster in some aspects of early language. The majority of girls talk earlier than boys, and nearly all girls string words together better, and earlier, than boys to make longer sentences, not just when they begin to talk but also in later life. They tend to read and write sooner than boys and their grammar and spelling is better, too. Girls also have better articulation, pronunciation and fewer reading problems at adolesence. Girls again are better at verbal reasoning than boys. Girls have fewer language disorders.

All the way up to adolescence girls are slightly better at arithmetic than boys, but then, after adolescence, boys show a slightly better score in tasks that use mathematical reasoning. Boys are better at almost every age at spatial visualization; they can move three dimensional objects around in their minds and better understand relationships in the physical world. This difference from girls becomes more pronounced and consistent all the way up to adolescence.

Socially, boys are much more aggressive and dominant than girls in all spheres, beginning in toddlerhood and continuing through to adolescence and later life if not checked. They are more competitive also – but this difference does not appear as early as aggression. Surprisingly, and hopefully, there is no gender difference in the desire to nurture.

Girls are undoubtedly more sociable, forming closer friendships, beginning as soon as they are socially aware, and continuing right through adolescence and adulthood. Girls also appear to be more compliant with adult requests in early childhood. Boys are more likely to show all forms of physical, emotional, and intellectual vulnerability to stress as well as more behavioural problems.

A knowledge of these gender differences can help parents to maximize their children's natural strengths and bolster their weak points. So you might introduce books early to a boy and play lots of word games as he grows up, paying special attention to pronunciation. With a girl, you might improve her spatial sense with an early formboard, jig-saw puzzles, snakes and ladders, and later chequers and chess. As soon as she is old enough, try a Rubik's cube.

The effect of stereotypes

Stereotypes of male and female roles will inevitably influence our children as they grow up if we are not sensitive to them and take appropriate avoiding action. All too early our children become affected by stereotyped concepts of appearance including body build, facial features, and clothes, and stereotyped concepts of behaviour and role playing, including approved speech, ways of expressing feelings and emotions, roles in marriage, earning a living, etc.

Parents have to be vigilant if we want our children to escape stereotyping. Stereotypes are dangerous; once accepted, they are used as yardsticks against which our children are judged – good and bad, successful and unsuccessful, appropriate and inappropriate – whereas we should be encouraging individuality and originality.

Worse, stereotypes can be used as guidelines for training children so that from earliest childhood, children are taught to think, feel, and act in line with a stereotyped model thereby stunting personal development. One of the worst aspects of stereotyping is the belief about superior and inferior roles, the former nearly always being male and the latter female.

Traditional sex-role stereotypes have little to recommend them whereas egalitarian sex-roles offer massive scope for self-realization and the belief that each child, regardless of gender, has to be encouraged to reach his or her own potential, irrespective of activity, and gain satisfaction without guilt, using his or her own abilities in whatever the chosen field.

As a parent, you have to act carefully from day one if you are to encourage a girl to be adventurous and strong, and a boy to be caring, able to show affection, and act as a peacemaker, especially as it's been proved that we handle pink-clothed babies differently from blue-clothed babies, and even use a different tone of voice.

PERSONALITY

Your child's personality can be described as having three main components: emotionality, which is a tendency to become upset or distressed easily and intensely, such children being very hard to soothe; activity, the amount of behaviour, which any baby shows in terms of movement, speed of talking, or the amount of energy put into any activities and restlessness; and sociability, the seeking to be especially gratified by rewards from social contact. Such children prefer to be with others and they like to share activities. They respond to others, and they seek responsiveness from others.

Your child's personality is a mixture of these three components in varying amounts, and even from the first few days of life it is possible to see that your child has a bias in one direction, being more emotional, more active or more sociable. Emotional babies tend to cry a lot and are not soothed easily; active babies tend to be restless and do not sleep very much; sociable babies can show their affection from the very first day of birth, responding to cuddles and being easily quietened.

If your child shows any one of these traits in excess it is up to you to accommodate it, but also to encourage your child to move in the direction of the other two. So for instance, if you have a very emotional child, your careful reassurance, support, guidance and help will help him feel secure and less emotional. Similarly, a child who seems to be in too much of a hurry all the time can be slowed down by your showing gentle restraint and lots of attention. Playing games with an active child will encourage him to concentrate and increase his attention span.

The development of personality

All parents hope that their child will grow up with a well-balanced personality, and it helps to know about the various stages that can be perceived as your child grows older. For instance, up to the age of one, what your child is doing is finding out whether the world can be trusted or mistrusted. The ideal result is that your baby learns to trust in mum or the person who looks after her. She also should learn to trust her own ability to make things happen. A key element to all this is that your baby is able to form an early secure attachment to you and/or your partner.

Between the ages of two and three a child's personality expands very quickly as he learns about his own will power and the possibility of dominating others through battles of will. At the same time, this is balanced out by creeping shame and doubt, as a result of each of control and physical incompetence. So learning to walk, grasping things and other physical skills lead to free choice, and as sphincter control occurs, a child learns control but may develop shame if accidents occur and he is blamed for them.

By four and five your child is learning about initiative versus guilt. Your child becomes capable of organizing activities around some goal, and becomes more assertive and aggressive, particularly if your child is a boy. Your child also develops a conflict with a parent of the same sex, and this may lead to guilt. Later, children concentrate on being industrious but have to cope with feelings of inferiority.

EMPATHY

Empathy is thinking about others and experiencing similar emotions to them. Healthy children show empathy quite early in their lives. During the first year, you will notice that your child responds in a rather global way to what is going on around her; so if she sees someone looking very unhappy, she may imitate the face, or if someone expresses a very strong emotion she will match that emotion herself. For instance she may begin to cry when she simply hears another infant crying, and babies commonly begin to cry if they see another one crying.

By about 12 to 18 months, when your child has a fairly clear sense of himself, he may respond to another person's distress by showing some distress of his own. He even may attempt to help the other person by offering what he finds most comforting for himself, and quite commonly, if your 18 month old sees another child hurt, he will come to get you to help.

A bit later, between the ages of two and three, your child will start to have empathy for another person's feelings and she will respond in a way that is much more to do with understanding the other person's situation rather than relating it to her own experience. Her empathetic responses become more and more subtle over the pre-school years as she becomes a better reader of other peoples' emotions.

Around four or five, your child's empathetic response becomes quite complicated in that it may take account of seeing contradictory emotions at the same time. So, if your little boy sees a friend fall over and get hurt, he will empathise not only with the hurt but also with the possible sense of shame or embarrassment that his friend will be experiencing and, instead of rushing to help, he may hang back because he knows that his friend would prefer not to be helped. A more generalised understanding of other peoples' feelings becomes apparent, which are not related simply to the immediate situation; you may find your child is sadder and more sympathetic to a friend's problem that extends into the long term than one that simply lasts a short time.

How you can help your child

The first task or crisis occurs during the first year of life when your child is developing a sense of trust in the predictability of the world and in her ability to affect the events around her. It is your behaviour that is critical to your child's successful or unsuccessful resolution of this crisis. Children who emerge from the first year with a firm sense of trust are those with parents who are loving and caring, and who respond predictably and reliably. In other words, a child who has developed a sense of trust will go on to form other relationships carrying this sense with her. Of course, it is important that your child develops some healthy mistrust as well, and learns to discriminate between dangerous situations and safe ones.

As your child becomes more mobile he develops a sense of independence or autonomy. Now if your child's efforts at independence are not carefully guided by you, he may experience repeated failures or ridicule, leading to a demoralization and a belief that he cannot succeed. This will mean that instead of having a feeling of basic self-control and self-worth, he may feel excessive shame about not being able to complete the tasks you set him.

Your four-year-old is able to plan a bit to take initiative, and to some degree responsibility. As your child tries out these new skills and tries to conquer the world, she will become aggressive. The risk is that your child may go too far and then you feel that you have to restrict and punish her. Too much of either of these things creates an imbalance producing guilt in your child.

By the time your child is six, she is concentrating on hard work and competence, and has the ability now to become a workaholic. Your task is simply to develop a repertoire of abilities that helps your child best cope with society's demands.

MALADJUSTMENT

Some undesirable personality traits appear in some form in all children. When they appear they seem harmless and usually we allow them to persist without any real effort to correct them. No single trait on its own is enough to cause alarm when viewed by itself – or even a few. The chart below shows some of the traits of a maladjusted child in descending order of frequency.

When there are more than a few maladjustments in the same child, however, they would seem to fit into a maladjusted personality picture and then they may be regarded as danger signals of future trouble. For example, most children fidget, but fidgeting on its own is

TYPICAL TRAITS OF A MALADJUSTED CHILD

☐ *Over active (this means aimless over-activity, NOT normal purposeful over-activity)*

☐ *Does not finish projects*

☐ *Fidgets*

☐ *Can't sit still at meals*

☐ *Does not stay with games*

☐ *Wears out toys, furniture*

☐ *Talks too much*

☐ *Does not follow directions*

☐ *Clumsy*

☐ *Fights with other children*

☐ *Unpredictable*

☐ *Teases*

☐ *Does not respond to discipline*

☐ *Gets into trouble*

☐ *Speech problems*

☐ *Temper tantrums*

☐ *Does not listen to whole story*

☐ *Defiant*

☐ *Hard to get to bed*

☐ *Irritable*

☐ *Reckless*

☐ *Unpopular with peers*

☐ *Impatient*

☐ *Tells lies*

☐ *Accident prone*

☐ *Wets the bed*

☐ *Destructive*

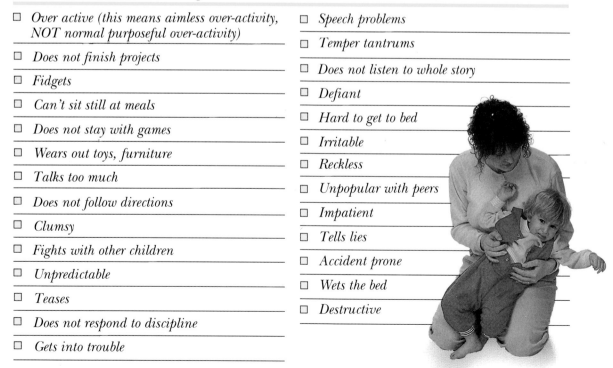

no cause for alarm unless there are other symptoms such as inability to concentrate, impatience, impulsivity or excessive aimless over-activity. With this array of traits there is cause for worry as all are symptomatic of poor personal and social adjustment.

But, just because your child may, for example, engage in one or more of these at different times, do not label him as a problem child. Bad habits like these are so common that many of them, especially if they only last a short time, should be considered part of normal development. For example, among seven year olds, 10 to 20 per cent still wet their beds at least occasionally, 30 per cent have nightmares, 20 per cent bite their fingernails, 10 per cent suck their thumbs, and 10 per cent swear enough for it to be considered a problem. Another 30 per cent or so have temper tantrums.

VULNERABILITY

Vulnerability is the term used by experts for your child's resilience, and a useful way to define it is in terms of the environment that will give your child sufficient support for optimum development. A resilient child is one for whom any of a very wide range of environments will support optimum development. In very simple terms, for a resilient child quite a few things going wrong will not hamper optimum development. On the other hand, a vulnerable infant is one with a narrow range of potentially supportive environments. For such a child, only the most stimulating, the most responsive, the most adaptive environments will do. In very simple terms, nearly everything must go right for him or her. When the child's environment falls outside that range the probability of a poor outcome is greatly increased.

Some babies are born with vulnerabilities, for instance low birth weight babies, pre-natally malnourished babies, or those who are temperamentally irritable babies; babies such as these will thrive only in highly supportive environments. Boys appear to be more vulnerable than girls, as they suffer more from stress.

Similarly, it is also possible that some babies are born more resilient. An interesting study done in Hawaii found that children reared in poverty, but who turned out well, were likely to have been easy or good-natured babies, and were probably the first born. Thus, an easy temperament may be one of the inborn characteristics that increases your child's resilience; other protective factors could include a secure attachment, a relatively high tolerance of frustration, and the ability to recover rapidly from disturbances.

All these things, however, can be helped by an understanding attitude in loving parents.

How you can help your child

An understanding of your child's vulnerability should make you think positively about her development because it means that even a vulnerable child can develop well if the environment in which she is growing up improves, and there is always room for improvement; improvement is always within your power to effect.

Just as importantly, the qualities of the environment that are critical for a child's optimum development change as the child grows up. Responsiveness and warm interactions with parents seem particularly crucial in the period between six to eighteen months, and the richness of mental and intellectual stimulation with toys, games, stories, songs, and parental attention are central between one and four years. The opportunity for practising social skills with peers, joining in games, sharing toys, making friends, is important at a still later age.

What parents should take most notice of is that the invulnerable child, the resilient child, the child who seems later to be able to cope best with life's stresses without lapsing into serious behaviour problems, has one very important thing going for her; she nearly always has at least one good strong secure relationship with a parent or with another caring adult. Such children are more successful at making relationships with their peers, have a better approach to solving problems (even as toddlers), and are better able to cope with life's stresses such as a parental divorce or a death in the family.

It would seem that this early secure attachment buffers the child against the problems and difficulties of normal life. In this respect, secure attachment is one of the best tools you can give your child to cope with life. A fundamental point for parents to bear in mind is that for a child to be able to handle temporary stresses without showing serious behaviour problems, she must have some close attachment but it need not be the first attachment at infancy. It can be an attachment that was formed with someone other than the parent later than the first year of life. This is one of the reasons why nannies, step-parents, grandparents, aunts and uncles, and even much older siblings can have a very important role to play in bringing up secure, happy children.

SECURITY OF ATTACHMENT

There is an enormous amount of research that shows the child who is secure develops in almost every way more successfully than the child who is insecure. Researchers have called these children "securely-attached." However, a frightening number of children are insecure in their infant years. Even in stable, happy, middle-class families, a third of all children are insecure.

The secure child is "unclingy" but, on the other hand, does not resist contact if you initiate it. If you have been absent for a while and are reunited with your secure baby, he will be very positive about greeting you and if upset, will be soothed by your presence and contact. A secure child always prefers you to a stranger. An insecure child, on the other hand, usually avoids contact with his mother, especially after being united after an absence. An even more insecure child is greatly upset when separated from his mum and it is impossible for her to comfort the child when she comes back. Such a child may even be angry when she returns and resists comfort from both her and a stranger. A severely insecure child may be apprehensive and confused, and will not like to be close to anyone; never making eye contact, never expressing emotion.

The positive effects of security are very easy to see in children at the age of two. For instance, secure toddlers have a longer attention span in play, they are more confident in trying to find solutions to tasks involving tools, and they often use mum as a source of assistance and as a problem solver in a very ready way. At eighteen to thirty months secure children have a more mature and complex play pattern showing that they are more sociable, intellectually advanced, and understand the world better than their insecure friends. Pre-school secure children have a faster and smoother interaction with a strange adult such as a teacher. Insecure children show many more behaviour abnormalities such as tantrums and aggressive behaviour. They are clinging, attention seeking, and at school badly behaved, getting attention by being naughty.

Secure children show more empathy towards other children and towards adults. They show no pleasure in other people's unhappiness; insecure children laugh at other people's distress. Around the age of four and five, securely attached children rate higher than insecure ones in terms of a flexible approach to life and resourcefulness, and secure children have a much higher self-esteem at the same age. Later on, at the age of five and six, secure children are more friendly and popular with their peers.

Why and how to promote security

It is in your best interests to promote security, to promote a secure attachment to you. There are very clear patterns of parental behaviour that promote security and these are the patterns that you should follow. The parents who have secure children match their behaviour to the child's, or follow the child's rhythm. Parents of secure babies also seem to be more likely to be emotionally outgoing towards their babies. They smile more, they use their voices more, and also use their voices in more expressive ways. They touch and hold their babies more.

In contrast, mothers of babies who are insecure are described as "psychologically unavailable". These mothers may be depressed and also dislike physical contact with their babies in the early months of life. These mothers tend not to give their babies attention and may even reject them, or avoid them.

STRESS

Very often the pace of today's life "hurries" children because it forces them to deal with separations and disturbing situations faster than they would comfortably. Young children perceive this type of "hurry" as personal rejection and as evidence that their parents do not really care about them. To a certain extent, hurrying children from one caretaker to another each day, or expecting too much from them, forcing them into academic achievement or making decisions that they are not really able to make, is a rejection. It is a rejection of the children as they see themselves and of what they are capable of coping with and doing. Being hurried affects not only a child's emotional well-being but his physical well-being, too. It also acts as a great drag on personal and, to some extent, physical growth.

Consider four-year-old Peter whose mother and father work. He is enrolled in a private nursery school and Peter is left with a neighbour each morning because his parents leave early. The neighbour prepares him for whoever is doing the school run that morning, who in turn takes him to school before 9 o'clock. At the end of the day this process is reversed and by the time he gets home Peter has been out of the house for almost twelve hours and has had to adapt to a number of different people and places. This is quite a strain for a four-year-old and Peter has to draw upon his energy reserves in order to cope. Not surprisingly at school he is a bit whiny and fussy and he does not seem that interested in playing with the other children. Occasionally he even sits just staring into space; he is clearly at the limit of his reserves and he is suffering from change overload.

All of us think that we adults have plenty of stresses to cope with in everday life but there is a scale of stresses in childrens' lives, too (see p88). Yearly scores below a 150 are average but children with scores between a 150 and 300 are almost certainly showing some symptoms of stress, like clingyness, behaviour problems, sleeplessness, inability to concentrate, being naughty at school, etc. If your child's score is above 300 there is a strong likelihood he is going through a serious health or emotional upset, and needs professional counselling.

Remember that play is nature's way of dealing with children's stress. As a parent you can help by investing in toys and play things that give the greatest scope to a child's imagination. Also remember that your child is learning from you all the time, particularly your actions and attitudes. So if you concentrate on the present and deal with what is worrying your child now, your child is likely to do the same. If you are a working parent, enjoy the time you spend with your child and try not to spoil it by dwelling on the times when you are not around and do not talk about the next separation. By worrying about the past and the future you lose the present and your children do not have you even when you are actually around them.

STRESS POINTS

☐ Parent dies	100		☐ Older sibling leaves home	29
☐ Parents divorce	73		☐ Trouble with grandparents	29
☐ Parents separate	65		☐ Outstanding achievement	28
☐ Parent travels as part of a job	63		☐ Move to another city	26
☐ Close family member dies	63		☐ Move to another part of town	26
☐ Personal illness or injury	53		☐ Receives or loses a pet	25
☐ Parent remarries	50		☐ Changes personal habits	24
☐ Parent fired from job	47		☐ Trouble with teacher	24
☐ Parents reconcile	45		☐ Change in child-care hours	20
☐ Mother goes to work	45		☐ Move to a new house	20
☐ Change in family member's health	44		☐ Changes to a new school	20
☐ Mother becomes pregnant	40		☐ Changes play habits	19
☐ School difficulties	39		☐ Vacations with family	19
☐ Birth of a sibling	39		☐ Changes friends	18
☐ New teacher or class	39		☐ Attends summer camp	17
☐ Change in family finances	38		☐ Changes sleeping habits	16
☐ Close friend is hurt or ill	37		☐ More or fewer family gatherings	15
☐ New extracurricular activity	36		☐ Changes eating habits	15
☐ Number of fights with siblings alter	35		☐ Changes amount of TV viewing	13
☐ Fears violence at school	31		☐ Birthday party	12
☐ Theft of personal possessions	30		☐ Punished for lying	11
☐ Changes in responsibilities at home	29			

PARENTAL SEPARATION AND DIVORCE

Children can experience emotional overload also, which can be caused by separation from people they love or trust. Children, of course, have to learn the pain of separation – that is a normal and healthy part of growth, but too much separation overstresses a child.

Parental separations and divorce "hurry" children because it forces them to deal with separations that they would not have to deal with until they were much older, say adolescents or young adults, forcing them to grow up prematurely. Other separations having the same effect would include a move to a new house, new friends and a new school. Divorce is particularly stressful because your child may be torn between you and the other parent as each of you could well be trying to win the child away from the other. Today, because divorce is so common, children sometimes feel stressed by even its possibility.

Divorce nearly always affects the same-sex children of the absent parent more than those children who stay with a parent of the same sex. A girl still has her mother to identify with if her father leaves home, but a boy who is without a father may never go through the identification process properly, and could end up with a very confused idea of his role and lack self-confidence and self-assurance.

All children show some short-term distress following a parental separation. In the first two years after a divorce children typically become more negative, more defiant, more depressed, angry and aggressive. Their school performance goes down and they may become ill more often. This disruption may go on for some time and one study found that five years after divorce about a third of children still showed significant disturbance including depression.

How you can help your child

The effects do seem to be greater for boys particularly in the short-term. Boys unfailingly show more distress, more negative and deviant behaviour, more school problems than girls from equivalent families. However, not all the news is bad. On the basis of research it looks as if in some circumstances children suffer lesser or shorter term effects. Children are less disturbed in the long term if their parents have little open conflict before the divorce and manage to remain civil after-wards. This includes the parents being able to agree on child rearing and discipline after the divorce and the children seeing the non-custodial parent, usually the father, regularly, thus maintaining a positive relationship with him. Maintaining a stable lifestyle in as many ways as possible for the children seems to help their adjustment to a divorce. This stability includes financial and emotional security and support for the custodial parent, usually the mother. Also staying in the same house and the same school, thus not having to adjust to many changes at once.

SIMPLE TESTS

SIMPLE TESTS

As a parent, being with your young child and observing him or her every day, you are in a unique position. In matters of wellbeing, you are your child's first line of defence and it is, therefore, up to you to monitor your child's development, and to be sensitive to anything out of the ordinary. Doctors traditionally depend on a parent's report in assessing a child, particularly because parents have information that others can't and the more knowledgeable you are about your child, the better service you can do him or her.

Whether as a result of one of these tests, or even through simple observation, you suspect something is not as it should be, don't hesitate to mention it to your doctor. The sooner a problem is dealt with, the better chance it can be corrected, and the more likely your child can still make the most of what he or she is capable. After the age of three, it is very difficult for even professionals to make up for any delays in learning.

What are the tests?

All the tests in the following section are adapted from ones that your health visitor, doctor or paediatrician would use if you took your child for a special check-up of his developmental milestones. They include tests of vision, hearing, observation, perception, intelligence, and a checklist of verbal skills. They should not be regarded as exams with the inevitable implication of failure and anxiety, but as informal check-ups. Certain assessments, like verifying your child's hearing and vision, are absolutely vital at an early stage as any impairment will affect his attainment of the skills necessary for normal development. Other tests, like those dealing with language and intelligence, can be used from time-to-time to check that your child is developing at an average rate, but assessment of giftedness is something that is best left to the more specialised tests of professionals. In any event, parents often are too unobjective to properly assess these areas.

There are also important areas of a child's development for which we have no recognised tests. These include things like sociability and personality development. However, even these can be monitored by parents using the development charts to devise their own tests.

But where there are recognised tests, I see no reason why knowledge of these should be kept from parents, not because you need to keep any kind of formal record, but so that you will know what to look out for, in order to readily spot warning signs and alert the experts early. Moreover, if you become knowledgeable about testing procedures, you will be better able to choose a properly qualified professional should their assistance be necessary, and will better understand the methods he or she might employ.

Interpreting the tests

The older the child, the more reliable the tests are bound to be, if for no other reason than the older child has a command of language that will enable him or her to follow instructions better. Also, except in certain areas such as hearing and vision, the results of any "test" that a child of less than a year may take cannot be regarded as predictive of future attainments.

So, it is very important that you don't regard the age-result ratio as written in stone. Your child is very unlikely to be spot on for every test; she'll be ahead in some, behind in others. On the whole, the tests are based on the outermost end of normal. For example, in the perception tests, I say a child of three should be able to name one colour. Most three-year-olds, of course, can name quite a few colours. However, if a three-year-old cannot name even one colour, there is certain to be a problem. Therefore, through the aid of this simple test, you could pick up a problem early. The action text will give you some guidelines as to what is outside of normal and this, rather than the suggested age range, should be the determining factor in seeking help. However, there probably is real cause for worrying if your child consistently and repeatedly scores very low on the tests.

It is important to bear in mind that balanced development is the best goal. A parent can, of course, work with a child to encourage precocity in a particular area. However, this is usually gained at the expense of progress in other, equally important, areas.

Administering the tests

If you are going to do any of the tests, start out with the attitude that they are meant to be fun, lots of laughs, and very relaxed. Do not force the pace or the duration. Pack in the test if your child appears bored or if it is certain that she will not cooperate. This is more likely to happen if unfamiliar people are involved in the testing.

Where tests require particular objects they are most often of the usual household variety or, if pictures, can be easily drawn or cut from magazines. Some of the observation tests, however, utilise shape, play or formboards, and these are obtainable from the sources listed on the back page.

Factors such as timing and the order of objects or sounds presented may be crucial, so try to follow the procedure exactly as it is set out. Most of the tests should be carried out in a quiet corner, free from distractions, so it will be easy for you to monitor responses.

You may want to repeat some of the tests, either because the initial results were inconclusive, or because you would like to monitor further development. This is also the practice among child development specialists. The important thing, though, is not to become obsessive about this testing, and to make certain it always remains a happy and fun-filled experience for you and your child.

DEVISING SIMPLE TESTS

The child-care professional has a variety of tests that he or she uses to assess development, and many of these, adapted for parental use, are set out in this chapter. But not all tests have to be formal, rigourous or involve continual assessment. Throughout the day, in caring for your child, you are in a position to make observations and receive useful feedback. For example, playtimes should allow you to monitor developing social skills, bathtimes afford an opportunity to assess curiosity and responsiveness, and mealtimes may provide evidence of mastery of manipulatory abilities. Seen this way, testing sessions will be spontaneous happenings, great fun, and occasions to enhance the strong bond that exists between you and your child.

WORKING WITH DEVELOPMENT CHARTS

It is possible also to construct your own tests for your child by using the charts for "The Normal Course of Development." As the charts are designed to show the progressive stages through which your child should pass, and not the precise times at which he should have attained specific skills, it is important to read the whole section of charts in order to get an overall idea of your child's progression. For example, to test your child's physical development, using the locomotion chart, the following should be borne in mind.

The goal of physical development is the ability to stand steadily on two legs, walk, run, and jump while maintaining balance and coordination. The first step on this pathway begins within the first month of life and starts with head control. From then on there are dramatic milestones during your child's development such as complete head control by 18 weeks, the ability to stand alone well by 14 months, walk backwards by 21 months, jump up and down by three years, and hop on one foot by five years, through which you can chart your child's progress. Remember some children are much slower at gaining physical skills than others, and achievement is very much dependent on your child's natural activity levels and how much you stimulate your child physically.

As long as you keep the overall pattern of development in mind you now can concentrate on the more specific aspects of each stage. If you look at the capsule information under each age, you can test the statements by doing what it says. For example at 32 weeks in manipulation a child can tear up paper. To test this activity offer him some tissue paper and see what he does with it.

On the following pages we have set out a more formal test/response checklist based on the information given in the "Locomotion" chart.

LOCOMOTION TESTS

MOBILITY

Procedure
Sit a short distance away from your baby and reach out your arms. Encourage him to come to you by calling out his name or offering him a favourite toy.

Response
By 32 weeks your baby may start to shuffle towards you on his bottom. Do not be alarmed if he cannot yet manage this. Rocking his body and reaching out are all preparatory to becoming mobile.

ABILITY TO STAND

Procedure
Offer your child your fingers to hold on to, to help him to pull himself up to sit and stand.

Response
By 40 weeks he should be able to pull himself into a sitting or standing position and, if able to hold on to stable pieces of furniture, should be happy and balanced standing. By about 13 months, having been practising with a mobile toy or round edged pieces of furniture for support, he should now have the confidence to stand alone unaided.

NECK AND BACK MUSCLE STRENGTH

Procedure
Lie your baby on his stomach and pass a coloured object, such as a toy, through his field of vision.

Response
Up to the age of four weeks your baby has little strength in his neck muscles. His eyes and head will follow the toy but he will be able to lift his head off the bed for only a few seconds. By the age of 12 weeks he should follow the toy with his head and be able to hold his head off the bed for an extended period. If the same test is done again at 24 weeks your baby will be able to lift himself and support himself on his forearms.

HEAD CONTROL

Procedure
Pull your child into a sitting position by her arms.

Response
At six weeks your baby's head will lag badly when she is pulled into a sitting position. By 12 to 16 weeks the lag will have lessened considerably, and by 20 weeks your child will have full head control and her head will not lag even when she rocks about.

ABILITY TO WALK

Procedure

Your child will start walking by shuffling sideways holding onto furniture, so move stable pieces of furniture together to see if she can start to move along them. Facing her, offer your hands as secure stabilisers, and see if she will yet start to walk forwards.

Response

By 48 weeks your child should walk sideways whilst holding onto furniture, and will walk forwards if both hands are held. By one year she will walk if you hold only one hand, and by 13 months may take her first independent step.

AGILITY

Procedure

Test your child's agility by demonstrating new activities such as walking backwards, hopping, jumping, rhythmic movement to music, and encouraging him to copy and join in.

Response

By 21 months your child should be able to walk backwards easily. By two years he should love rhythmic movements and should get great pleasure from dancing and swaying to music, clapping hands and singing. By two and a half he should be capable of jumping and walking on tip-toe games, and by three should be able to hop and enjoy 'hopscotch' and physical games such as *Simon Says*.

MANOEUVRABILITY AND MUSCULAR CO-ORDINATION

Procedure

Test adventurousness, muscular co-ordination and manoeuvrability by providing access to outdoor equipment and toys such as skates, skate boards or stilts.

Response

By three years your child should have strong enough calf muscles and enough flexibility in her feet to be able to ride a bicycle. By four years old your child should be very active and should be able to perform activities which depend on muscle co-ordination such as skipping, hopping, jumping and climbing on a climbing frame. By five years old her muscle co-ordination is finely developed and she will enjoy large outdoor apparatus and be able to practise her movement on skates and stilts, although she will only be able to perform for a short while.

ACHIEVEMENT VARIATIONS

Remember that these are average ages at which certain developments occur, and your child will probably develop these skills at an earlier or later stage. Experts usually give a large allowance for late development before considering a child's development pattern to be abnormal. However, should your child show a serious deviation from this development pattern, you should consult your doctor.

TESTING TASTE

Taste buds on the tongue detect four basic tastes: sweet, sour, bitter and salty. Newborn babies respond differently to all four flavours. When newborn infants are fed flavoured water they seem to make characteristic facial expressions in response to certain tastes. Very dilute bitters dropped onto a newborn's tongue will cause him to open his mouth wide – as though in shock! The fact that babies show such distinctive expressions tells us that different flavours do indeed taste different to your baby. If you like, you can test your baby's primitive responses, although giving him bitters is not recommended as he will find it unpleasant.

TESTS UP TO THE AGE OF FOUR WEEKS OLD

SWEETNESS

Procedure
Using a baby dropper, dispense a couple of drops of sugar water on your baby's tongue.

Response
Your baby's face should relax, and will take up an expression which looks a lot like a smile.

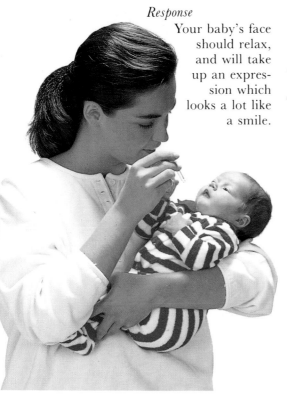

SALTINESS

Procedure
Place a salt-coated finger in your baby's mouth.

Response
Your baby will make a grimace, and will push your finger out of his mouth.

SOURNESS

Procedure
Put two drops of very dilute lemon juice on your baby's tongue.

Response
Your baby will close her eyes, purse her lips, and screw up her face and may even give a little shudder.

Action
There is no need to consult a doctor unless your baby is not registering response to different tasting food by about the age of 24 weeks, when mixed feeding has been established for six or eight weeks. Defects in the senses of taste and smell are very rare indeed but consult your doctor if you need reassurance.

TESTING HEARING

For a child to be able to speak correctly, he needs to be able to hear the range of sound cycles that are essential for speech. Until your child proves that he hears, later that he imitates, and eventually that he can correctly use the individual phonetic units of speech, you can't be certain that his auditory discrimination is normal. With older children the proof is how they respond to spoken language (see overleaf), but with smaller babies, you have to judge by the way they respond to different sounds (see test, right). With a baby aged six months onwards, spontaneous vocalisations provide useful clues to his capacity for hearing and using spoken language. Such sounds should be carefully observed and recorded. There are also various clues to hearing that you should be aware of during the first year (see the list below).

On the following pages are set out some sample hearing tests for children up to three. You and your child should find them fun, but for the most accurate results it is necessary that you carry them out in a quiet room, and you or some other familiar adult must be present at all times. You should carefully follow the procedure – as in which order to say or touch things, or present certain objects, and you should note carefully the distances used, the results obtained, and anything you might say during the tests. Should you be concerned about the outcome, you will want to share this information with your doctor as soon as possible.

CAN YOUR BABY HEAR YOU?

Here is a checklist of some signs you can look for in your baby's first year:

Newborn

Your baby should be startled by a sudden loud noise such as a hand clap or a door slamming, and should blink or open his eyes widely to such sounds.

By four weeks

Your baby should be beginning to notice sudden prolonged sounds like the noise of the vacuum cleaner.

By 16 weeks

He should quieten or smile at the sound of your voice even when he cannot see you. He may also turn his head or eyes towards you.

By 28 weeks

He should turn immediately to your voice across the room, or to very quiet noises made on each side.

By 36 weeks

He should listen attentively to familiar everyday sounds and search for very quiet sounds made out of sight. He should also show pleasure in babbling.

By one year

He should show some response to his own name and to other familiar words. He may also respond when you tell him "no" and "bye bye".

HEARING TESTS

24 WEEKS TO 18 MONTHS

Preparation

Any adult can perform the test but the baby should sit on a parent's lap. He or she should be no closer than 4 feet (1.2 m) to any wall. The tester should stand well to the side of the baby and outside her immediate range of vision. For a 24-week-old baby, stand 18 inches (45 cm) away from her ear, and level with it; for a 36-week-old or older baby, stand 3 feet (90 cm) away.

Soft high-pitched rattle

Squares of new tissue paper (hard toilet paper)

Small handbell

China or pottery cup with wide brim, and metal spoon

Procedure

Make sounds in the following order: voice ("OO" – low pitched; "PS" – high pitched), rattle, spoon against cup, tissue paper, handbell. Try each sound on both ears. If you get no response the first time you make the sound, wait two seconds and repeat it. Then wait a further two seconds as she may still respond. If there is no response after three tries, try the next sound.

Response

Normal children of 36 weeks upwards, on first hearing the sound, will usually turn instantly, and very often smile as they do so. Younger babies may be slower to respond.

Action

A clear-cut response to any three of these five sounds means your baby probably possesses enough hearing to speak. If the response is less repeat the test within two weeks and consult your clinic if in any doubt.

Keep bell out of baby's vision

18 MONTHS TO TWO YEARS

Preparation

Put a ball, toy car, cup and spoon, baby doll and a 1-inch (2.5 cm) brick of a different colour from the car on a low table and sit your child at the table with yourself opposite 2–3 feet (60–90 cm) away, i.e. normal conversational distance. Have another familiar person on hand.

Procedure

Introduce all the toys one by one to your child. For example, "This is a car." Then hold your hand out flat, so that the shape of it does not suggest the object that you are expecting to receive, and say, "Give me the ball ... brick ... car ... dolly," in this order.

If your child does this correctly, give the cup to the other person, Daddy for instance, and tell your child you will ask him to give the toys to the other person. Move to six feet (1.8 m) away and ask your child to give Daddy the ball ... then move further away, up to ten feet (3 m), giving the other commands. Finally, ask your child to put the things in the cup and bring them to you. Many normal children at this age find it very difficult to communicate properly at a distance of ten feet (3 m). If you feel you have gone too far away, move back to 6 feet (1.8 m) away, and see if your child will do what you ask.

Response

If your child does not respond the first time, wait for a little while as it may just be a delayed response. He may even lift the incorrect toy, put it down, and pick up the correct one. If he gives you the incorrect toy, gently put it down and repeat the command. If he persistently gives the wrong toys, or goes on giving all the other toys without being given a command, just accept them. At some time when your child is distracted, make a high-pitched vocal noise, rattle something, or rustle paper as for babies one year to 18 months, to make sure that he responds by turning.

Action

If the response is uncertain and there is reason to doubt that your child's hearing is normal, have him seen by a doctor without delay.

TWO TO THREE YEARS

Preparation

Sit your child opposite you at the table with a cup, spoon, ball, car, doll and brick set out as for 18 months to two years. Make sure you have a piece of card to hand to hide your lips for part of the test.

Procedure

Introduce all the toys as follows: cup, spoon, ball, car, doll, and brick. Ask your child to hand them to you one by one. Then put the spoon in the cup, saying, "I'm putting the spoon in the cup."

Now move to 6 feet (1.8 m) away and hide your mouth slightly with the card so that your child can't read your lips. In a quiet, conversational tone of voice, ask her to put the toys in the cup one by one. Then move to 10 feet (3 m) away and ask her to take them out again, all except one. Ask her what is left in the cup.

Response

If your child does not respond to this test then try a simple conversation, or, if that is too difficult, point to and name some objects. The following simple vocabulary list will test for recognition of most of the common vowels and consonants: doll, shoe, nose, dress, arm, feet, hair, hand, mouth, eyes, teeth.

Action

If your child's hearing appears normal but she is not able to put words together to form complicated sentences and is not engaging in spontaneous verbal exchange with you or others, she should be seen by a professional.

TESTING VERBAL SKILLS

Whatever you do, do not confuse lateness in the development of speech with lateness in learning to speak distinctly. Lateness in developing speech means lateness in beginning to say single words with meaning, and after that putting two or three words together with meaning. Distinct speech is something that emerges gradually and mild speech defects are very common in young children.

Causes of speech retardation

The commonest form of indistinct speech is the lisp, a phase which many babies go through when they are starting to learn to talk. It is due to the protrusion of the tongue between the teeth when the letter "s" is being said and nearly always disappears without treatment, but you can help your child to avoid this defect by making him aware of his tongue and its movements by giving him foods which need to be licked or sucked.

Probably the commonest cause of lateness in developing speech is a child's not being spoken to, sung to, or played with. All children have a natural desire to join in human activities, and if you speak to your child a great deal, he will have an enormous desire to join in your conversation. This is one of the best ways of encouraging speech development.

Before you become anxious about late speech development ask your husband and members of your family how quick they were to speak because quite often there is a family history of a lateness in speech development.

Bear in mind that girls tend to speak earlier than boys, and bilingualism does not delay speech.

If we take late speakers as a whole there is a characteristic family environment with greater emotional instability, a desire for greater perfectionism, parents who restrict activities and independence, and nearly always some over-protectiveness. In this kind of home there tends to be confusion and tension. Parental disapproval and criticism may also retard speech development and very often a child's speech regresses when a new baby arrives.

Even if you have other children, do not depend on them to teach your child to speak; a child learns speech more from parents than brothers and sisters. Either parent can greatly help their child in speech development by talking to her and reading to her.

Deafness can lead to late development of speech and this is why testing for hearing (see p98) is very important. A baby will not learn to speak if she is deaf. Tongue-tie, unless it is really very severe, does not interfere with speech development. Child abuse almost always delays speech development.

Some early milestones in language development

Researchers have provided 57 language milestones spanning the first three years of life. All of them have been selected because of their significance as markers of linguistic development.

Language refers to any system for the storage or exchange of information. It therefore, encompasses not only speech but listening, comprehension, and communication by visual means – such as smiling, or recognising familiar persons or objects. Even the imitation or initiation of gestures may be language phenomena.

Checklist of language milestones

The checklist (see opposite) has been divided into three sections, auditory expressive (early vocalisation, naming of objects, etc.), auditory receptive (response to sounds, words and commands, etc.), and visual, largely so that a distinction can be made between auditory, visual, and verbal causes of language retardation. Some children may be unable to form words properly, but have normal hearing comprehension and normal visual communication skills. On the other hand, a deaf child may have delayed speech because of impaired auditory comprehension, but retains normal visual communication skills. So the tests have been devised to screen out the various aspects of language delay. Remember the ages indicated are averages, meaning that your baby will acquire any skill earlier or later than the time shown, never spot on.

Results of tests

A completely non-vocal baby is cause for concern and may need several kinds of testing including hearing tests (see p98). If your baby remains silent in the first few months consult your doctor or health visitor as soon as you become concerned.

The emergence of your baby's first word is crucial, but the range of normal is very wide. If your baby can say one word with meaning by the age of two there is probably nothing to worry about if more words follow. If, on the other hand, your child is making sounds but is still wordless at two and a half, you should consult your doctor or the local department of speech therapy.

Infantile speech patterns such as a lisp or slight stutter are acceptable up to age four, but persistent and marked indistinct speech should be treated by a speech therapist.

For more information on speech impairment please see p167, The Special Child.

EARLY LANGUAGE MILESTONES AT AVERAGE AGE IN MONTHS

AUDITORY EXPRESSIVE

☐ Coos	3.2
☐ Makes sounds back to you	2.6
☐ Laughs	4.0
☐ Blows bubbles (gives "raspberry")	7.3
☐ Monosyllabic babbling (dadadada)	10.0
☐ Polysyllabic babbling (umengooka)	10.8
☐ Mama/Dada: non-specific usage	10.1
☐ Mama/Dada: correct usage	14.0
☐ First word beyond mama/dada	17.0
☐ 4-6 single words	23.5
☐ Tells 2 or more wants	20.8
☐ 2 word sentences	23.2
☐ 50 or more single words	25.6
☐ Any use of "me" or "you"	28.8
☐ Uses prepositions	34.2
☐ Holds brief conversation	34.3
☐ Gives name and use of two objects	34.4
☐ Correct use of pronoun "I"	36

AUDITORY RECEPTIVE

☐ Alerts to voice	1.0
☐ Turns laterally to voice	2.9
☐ Recognises certain sounds	3.1
☐ Turns laterally to bell	5.0
☐ Turns laterally then downward to bell	8.2
☐ Inhibits action on command "no"	10.1

☐ Follows one-step commands	13.5
☐ Follows two-step commands	25.1
☐ Points to named object	27.0
☐ Points to objects described by use	32.6
☐ Follows prepositional commands	36

VISUAL

☐ Smiles	1.5
☐ Recognizes parents	2.9
☐ Recognizes objects	2.9
☐ Responds to facial expressions	4.7
☐ Visual tracking	4.7
☐ Blink to threat	4.9
☐ Imitates gesture games	9.1
☐ Follows gestural commands	11.0
☐ Initiates gesture games	12.0
☐ Points to desired objects	17.0

TESTING INTELLIGENCE

In 1905, the first modern intelligence test was published by two Frenchmen. It was done at the request of the French Government who sought a way of identifying children who would be likely to have problems in school. From the very beginning therefore, the test was based on the assumption that children differed in mental ability and it had the purpose of predicting school success. This predictive aspect of IQ testing is one which remains today.

Defining intelligence

Because the original investigators defined intelligence as including judgement, comprehension, and reasoning, the tests they devised were very much like some school tasks including measures of vocabulary or word power, the comprehension of facts and relationships, and mathematical and verbal reasoning. So the sort of questions that were asked were, can a child describe the difference between wood and glass? Can the young child touch his nose, his ear, and his head? Can the young child tell which of two weights is heavier? All of these tests were ways of measuring individual differences in intellectual power.

The "power" definition of intelligence has held sway for many years. One of its greatest weaknesses is that it ignores the fact that intelligence incontrovertibly develops over time. So, for instance, your five year old will have great difficulty making a mental list of things to buy at the supermarket. Your eight year old will remember things more easily, rehearsing the list under his breath or in his head while he walks to the store. At ten years old, your child will use mental strategies, techniques, and types of logic to increase his recall. So a later theory of intelligence takes account of these learning processes, and the focus shifts to the development of thinking structures, rather than thinking power, and therefore on patterns of development that are common to all children rather than stressing individual differences -- a much more positive approach.

Assessing Intelligence

The most modern approach to intelligence testing is to view intelligence as the ability to process information, and therefore concentrates on understanding the building blocks of thinking, such as improving memory, or encouraging planning strategies. What we then test is something much more rational – that is, how speedily a child acquires thinking skills and applies them to everyday life. With a very young or pre-school child intelligence testing is dependent on other aspects of development, such as the acquisition of language and manipulative skills. Professional tests only begin to be predictive from the age of 30 months onwards.

What you can do to help

As a parent you should accept your child's intelligence and not push it beyond its limits but also not undervalue it; regard it as a quality that can be developed by careful teaching with an accent on stimulation and gentle stretching of thinking processes. Testing for IQ is totally uncompetitive, and you should not compare your child with any other. Comparison with other children is simply not allowable because children who have the same IQ score may well vary in their performance of individual tests, and therefore require completely different help. Neither should you interpret an IQ test in isolation; it doesn't take account of creativity or artistic talent. You have to accept your child for who he or she is, in the knowledge that with the correct guidance and support you can optimise the development of your child's intelligence.

If you have a child whose intelligence falls outside of the normal border lines whether high or low, he is going to need special attention and of that you must be aware (see p158, The Special Child). To give you some idea of the distribution of intelligence throughout the population, very few children are retarded and very few at the other end of the scale are gifted. Your child is almost certainly in the middle and you must fit your expectations to that.

The case against IQ tests

It is only fair to give you the arguments against using IQ tests, particularly in schools. The first is that they measure certain sorts of skills needed in schools but they do not tap a whole range of other skills that are equally important for success in life.

IQ tests may label a child as slow or retarded but ignore other important skills that compensate for the inability simply to do IQ tests well.

Most IQ tests have a bias and they are nearly always biased against groups of children who are underprivileged in terms of life experience. An example of this would be the question "What is the thing you do if another child hits you without meaning to?". The answer that gets top marks is "walk away", but if you come from a neighbourhood where greater store is laid on courage, where you stay and confront the child or even hit him back, the answer "walk away" has no relevance, and the child who gives the answer "hit him back" would be underscored.

IQ tests are very often loosely used to predict how successful a child will be in later life, and, as intelligence develops over time, and according to experience and stimulation, this is an entirely unfair application.

Many teachers fall prey to the aspect of the self-fulfilling prophecy of an IQ test score and it is very hard for a child to escape the initial categorisation.

IQ TESTS

UP TO 12 WEEKS

Procedure
Dangle a ring in front of your child.

Response
Your child should reach for the dangling ring.

32 WEEKS

Procedure
While playing, hide a toy under a cloth.

Response
Your child should uncover the toy that has been hidden by the cloth.

36 WEEKS

Procedure
Take a basket and some cubes and ask your child to place the cubes in the basket. If your child does not respond at first you can show her how to put the cubes in the basket while describing what you are doing.

Response
Your child should put the cubes into the basket.

15 MONTHS

Procedure
Ask or show your child how to build a tower of three cubes, one on top of another.

Response
Your child should be able to build a tower of three blocks each balancing on the other without it falling over.

AGE THREE ONWARDS

The Wechsler Intelligence Scale for children from three upwards involves ten types of tests divided into two groups – those that rely on verbal abilities and those on performance. The latter tests do not concentrate on language ability, and test your child's perceptual skills and logic.

Although performance increases with age, gifted children do well on all the tests, and retarded children do badly on all the tests, though they may do somewhat better on performance tests than verbal tests. The key point is that most children show an unevenness in doing them, and this could alert you to an area that needs specific help.

Tests such as these are normally given by experts, and need interpreting by them for a completely accurate result. However, you might like to try some if you're at all worried about your child's development. Then should he or she need testing, you'll be more familiar with the procedure.

VERBAL TESTS
These are divided into categories and include:

General information: How many eyes have you?

General Comprehension: What is the thing you do when you scrape your knee?

Arithmetic: James had ten marbles and he bought four more. How many marbles did he have altogether?

Similarities: In what way are a pear and an orange alike?

Vocabulary: What is an emerald?

PERFORMANCE TESTS
These are divided into five categories – picture completion, picture arrangement, block design, object assembly, and coding – and are illustrated opposite.

Picture completion

Show your child pictures of familiar objects in which a part has been left out. Your child should identify the missing part, such as the eye missing from a bunny.

Picture arrangement

Lay out a strip of pictures like those in a comic in the wrong order. Your child should arrange them correctly to make a story.

Coding

Show a series of symbols like rings, stars, diamonds, and triangles – two of each. Your child has to pick out the symbols that go together.

Object assembly

Cut up a large picture of a familiar object – a face or a horse – into pieces like a simplified jigsaw. Your child has to put them together in the right configuration as quickly as possible.

Block design

Use sets of special blocks (red, white, half red, half white) and ask your child to copy designs that you demonstrate first. At first use only four blocks, but as she gets older, use up to nine.

TESTING OBSERVATION

Your baby's powers of observation are the summation of various different aspects of development, including mental development, vision and general understanding, and are evident before the age of 24 weeks. For instance, at that age if you place a piece of wool or string on the floor in front of your sitting baby, she will look for it, notice it, recognise it, and reach out for it, even though she may not be able to pick it up yet.

The ideal age for testing to begin is probably around 15 months, but there are tests you can do somewhat earlier than that though any tests before the age of six months are extremely questionable. Many of our tests use special boards available by post (see p192).

OBSERVATION TESTS

15 MONTHS TO 3 YEARS

	Age	Action
☐	*15 months*	*Inserts round block without being shown*
☐	*18 months*	*Piles three blocks one on top of the other*
☐	*2 years*	*Places all three in the correct places occasionally making errors and correcting them.*

	Age	Action
☐	*2 ½ years*	*Inserts all three forms adapting quickly after any error.*
☐	*3 years*	*Inserts all three forms with no error or immediate correction.*

This test uses a simple formboard of only three shapes.

2 1/2 TO 4 YEARS

Age	Action
☐ 2½ years	*places 1 shape*
☐ 3 years	*places 3 shapes*
☐ 4 years	*places all shapes*

Board of plain background and vari-coloured shapes

3 TO 5 YEARS

Age	Action
☐ 3 years	*places 4 shapes*
☐ 3½ years	*places 6 shapes*
☐ 4 years	*places 8 shapes*
☐ 4½ years	*places 9 shapes*
☐ 5 years	*places all shapes*

One-colour formboard of 12 shapes

Pictorial representations
or actual common objects
can be used

18 MONTHS TO 3½ YEARS

Age	Action
☐ 18 months	points to 1 common object
☐ 2 years	points to 1, names 3 common objects
☐ 2½ years	points to 7, names 5 common objects
☐ 3 years	names 8 common objects
☐ 3½ years	names 10 common objects

3 YEARS TO 5 YEARS

Age		Action
☐ 3 years		names one colour
☐ 4 years		names 2 or 3 colours
☐ 5 years		names 4 colours

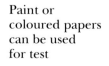

Paint or
coloured papers
can be used
for test

3½ TO 7 YEARS

Using this more complicated formboard, measure the length of time your child takes to complete the test. As she gets older she gets much faster at it.

Age	Time
☐ 3 ½ years	*56 seconds*
☐ 4 years	*46 seconds*
☐ 5 ½ years	*40 seconds*
☐ 5 years	*35 seconds*
☐ 6 years	*27 seconds*
☐ 7 years	*23 seconds*

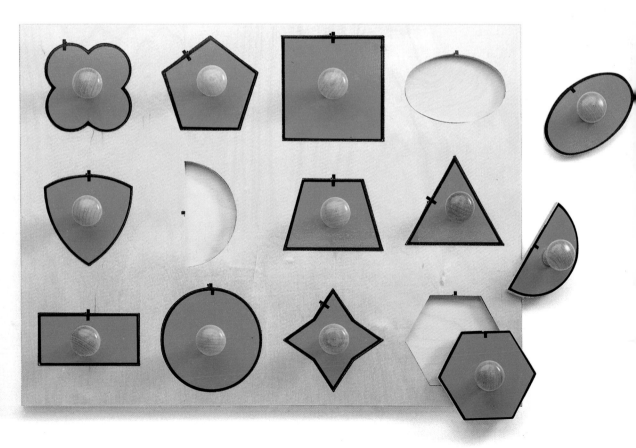

FROM THREE YEARS

Procedure

Draw an incomplete person and ask your child to complete it. When he's finished, go over the drawing discussing what he's added and asking him what else is missing. Put the parts in together.

Response

Your child's drawing will get more and more complicated with age. Expect one to two parts at three years, three parts at four years, six parts at four and a half years, six or seven parts at five years and eight parts at six years.

THREE AND A HALF YEARS ONWARDS

Procedure

Ask your child to draw a person and urge her to draw it carefully the best way she can and to take as much time as she likes. Your child receives one point for each of the items, listed in the chart opposite, which is present in her drawing. For each four points one year is added to her basic age which is taken as three. Thus, if your child's drawing shows nine items she scores nine points and therefore her mental age score, and her power of observation, is five and a quarter years.

Action

Some children are naturally observant but you can encourage your child to take in detail by constantly pointing them out. Draw your child's attention to colours, smells, shapes, and textures in finer and finer detail. Point out birds, plants, aeroplanes, butterflies – indeed anything moving, and then talk about them.

AWARD ONE POINT FOR:

- ☐ *Head present*
- ☐ *Legs present*
- ☐ *Arms present*
- ☐ *Trunk present*
- ☐ *Length of trunk greater than breadth*
- ☐ *Shoulders being indicated; both arms and legs attached at the trunk*
- ☐ *Legs attached to the trunk at correct point*
- ☐ *Arms attached to the trunk at correct point*
- ☐ *Neck present*
- ☐ *Neck outline continuous with head or trunk*
- ☐ *Eyes present*
- ☐ *Nose present*
- ☐ *Mouth present*
- ☐ *Nose and mouth in two dimensions; two lips showing*
- ☐ *Nostrils indicated*
- ☐ *Hair shown*
- ☐ *Hair over more than head circumference*
- ☐ *Clothing present*
- ☐ *Two articles of non-transparent clothing*
- ☐ *Both sleeves and trousers shown*
- ☐ *Four or more articles of clothing definitely indicated*
- ☐ *Costume complete without incongruities*
- ☐ *Fingers shown*
- ☐ *Correct number of fingers shown*
- ☐ *Fingers shown in two dimensions*
- ☐ *Finger length greater than breadth*
- ☐ *Opposition of thumb shown*
- ☐ *Hands down*
- ☐ *Hands shown distinct from fingers or arms*
- ☐ *Arm joint shown; elbow, shoulder or both*
- ☐ *Leg joint shown; knee, hip or both*
- ☐ *Head in proportion*
- ☐ *Arms in proportion*
- ☐ *Legs in proportion*
- ☐ *Feet in proportion*
- ☐ *Both arms and legs shown in two dimensions*
- ☐ *Heel shown*
- ☐ *Firm lines without overlapping at junctions*
- ☐ *Firm lines with correct joining*
- ☐ *Head outline more than a circle*
- ☐ *Trunk outline more than a circle*
- ☐ *Outline of arms and legs without narrowing at junction with body*
- ☐ *Features symmetrical and in correct position*
- ☐ *Ears present*
- ☐ *Ears in correct position and proportion*
- ☐ *Eyebrows or lashes present*
- ☐ *Pupil of eye present*
- ☐ *Eye length greater than height*
- ☐ *Eye glance directed to front in profile*
- ☐ *Both chin and forehead shown*
- ☐ *Profile with not more than one error*

TESTING PERCEPTION

A young baby is surrounded by buzzing confusion because it is not possible for him to single out sights and sounds in the world around him. As he gets older, however, he becomes more adapted to his setting, and can focus on sights and sounds in ever clearer detail.

An infant starts to do this in the first weeks and if there is a particular stimulation in a quiet background, you will notice that your young baby is "captured" by the stimulation. This means that your baby's powers of perception are taking up a purposefulness, which you can help develop.

Helping your child

Initially your baby will focus on prominent features like your eyes, and your moving mouth, and your wriggling fingers, or a toy being swung in front of her. As your child grows older she will focus on more and more detail, and start to make distinctions that are quite difficult, such as the difference in size between two bricks, and therefore the size of grasp in order to pick each one up.

After several months your child becomes more and more efficient by focusing on those details that are essential, and ignoring the rest. For instance, your child knows that she must focus on your voice, and will do so even in a noisy setting.

The sense of touch is one of the first centres for exploration so it is important to introduce your young baby to different textures like smooth, rough, and furry, and different shapes like round and square. This helps him to examine and know his world by relating his visual perceptions to those of other senses like touch. You can develop your baby's perception if you demonstrate what follows on from a certain shape. Show your baby a ball, rub his fingers over it so that he feels the smooth texture of the ball and then roll it towards him (you can do this with a balloon when your baby is very young, indeed as young as two weeks if propped up with cushions). Your baby will perceive roundness in some detail, and you are teaching him the meaning of this information.

You can help your child to focus on important information and shut off less important information by directing her attention with your own interest, like demonstrating what a toy can do in your child's field of vision, pointing out bright colours, illustrating interesting shapes, and as early as possible "reading" books with your child, pointing out pictures and objects, and naming things. This way you will help your child become steadily better at identifying what is irrelevant so that she learns to ignore it, a very important attribute for your child to master if she is going to be able to concentrate and have a long attention span.

PERCEPTION TESTS

16 WEEKS

This very simple test demonstrates that your baby is able to make certain distinctions like small rather than big.

Procedure
Draw a small circle over a large circle on a piece of card and show it to your baby. Follow this with a card on which is drawn a small diamond on top of a large diamond, your baby should get the relationship between the small shape over the large shape.

Response
Now show your baby a card on which there is drawn a small triangle on top of a large triangle. If your baby has got the idea of small over big from the previous two cards, he will not show any interest at all in this picture. If, however, you him show him a card on which there is a large triangle over a small triangle, a different thing altogether, he will show renewed interest in the fourth card.

24 TO 36 WEEKS

By this age babies have depth perception and you can test this in the following way, making sure that you are careful not to let your baby slip or fall.

Procedure
Put your baby onto a sofa or a table that is about 18 inches (45cm) from the ground, and with you there to protect her, let her move on the surface.

Response
Your baby will crawl right to the edge but then stop, and will not go over the edge, showing that she can see there is a difference in height between the surface she is on and the surface below her, onto which she will fall if she crawls over the edge.

36 WEEKS ONWARDS

By this time your baby has a conception of "object permanence", which is the understanding that an object exists even though he cannot see it or it is hidden from view. Up to this age a baby will show no signs of searching for a toy if he drops it over the edge of his chair. From 32 or 36 weeks your baby will look over the edge to look for the dropped toy.

Procedure
Practise letting your child reach for a toy that is placed on a surface in front of him. After he has reached for the toy several times, replace the toy and put a bit of paper between the baby and the toy.

Response
Your baby will try to move the paper out of the way to find the toy that he knows is still there. Your baby will go on searching until he has found the toy.

18 MONTHS

From the age of about 24 weeks onwards your child will have been developing her own "perceptual style," which is dependent on the speed or care with which your baby examines objects or situations; this is called "conceptual tempo". A slow tempo baby will remain still and look at something with fixed concentration. This child is called reflective. A fast tempo baby, however, will become excited, gurgle, and thrash around and look away after only a short period of examination. This child is called impulsive.

By the age of eighteen months you can get some idea of your child's "reflection versus impulsivity" by trying out a simple test.

Procedure

Show your baby a card on which there are slight variations of the same picture. Your baby is going to select the picture from among the bottom six that exactly matches the figure at the top.

If your baby is a reflective child, she will look carefully at all the alternatives before making a choice, and she will make few errors.

If your child is an impulsive child on the other hand, she will look at all the objects quickly and choose one that is quite often inaccurate.

It is very unlikely that your child will fit neatly into this category system; in addition to fast inaccurates and slow accurates, there are fast accurates and slow inaccurates.

Action

It would be quite wrong if you expected to change the kind of child you have, but if you do this test it will help you to be more realistic about what you expect from your child. For instance, it has been shown that reflective children have a somewhat easier time learning to read, which when you think about it makes sense of the sort of careful examination of letter forms that is needed in the early stages of reading. In conventional lessons at school more reflective skills are demanded, so reflective children may do slightly better at school than impulsive ones.

Reflectiveness, however, is not always best. There are many situations in life when you have to make a very rapid decision. When your child goes out into the street for instance and practises road drill, she has to make decisions about about moving traffic, clear spaces, and when to cross, and sometimes is given a very short time in which to make this decision. It could be that impulsive children do this better than reflective ones. There are also times of course when it helps if a simple glance is enough and an impulsive child will then have the advantage over a reflective one.

THREE YEARS ONWARDS

Perceptual style can also be described in terms of your child's ability to be heavily influenced by the background environment or being able to ignore it. This is called field dependency or field independency.

Measurements made of field independence/dependence do show a sex difference in that boys are more field independent, and therefore can pick out a shape from a complicated background more easily than girls who are field dependent. This could be because boys are better at spatial visualization from a much earlier age than girls.

You can test your child for field independence/dependence by seeing whether or not he is able to pick out one of several single basic geometrical shapes from a more complicated drawing.

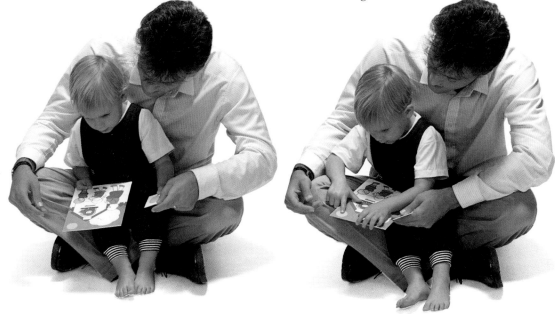

Procedure
Show your baby a simple geometrical figure such as a circle, square or a triangle, and then ask him to find the figure exactly like that one in a more complex drawing.

Response
Your child may be able to find the shape in the picture. In order to find the figure your child has to ignore other features of the drawing (the field) and pay attention only to abstract shapes. Generally speaking children become more and more field independent as they get older. Then, you can introduce more complicated shapes – a hidden animal, for example – in more complicated backgrounds.

Action
It will be helpful for you to know if your child is field independent. If so he will generally be able to focus his attention more successfully on objects or tasks, while field-dependent children tend to focus more on people; this may account for why girl babies, who are more field dependent, are more sociable from the very outset. If your child is field dependent, he will rely more on outside cues, and therefore, on your prompting and your encouragement. In contrast, however, your field independent child, because of his greater ability to extract parts from wholes, will tend to be better at some cognitive tasks such as those that require spatial visualization, i.e. playing chess.

TESTING VISION

Visual acuity refers to how clearly you can see somebody; 20/20 vision is normal. Newborn babies have quite poor acuity, perhaps as poor as 20/800, but it improves rapidly during early infancy so that most 16 week olds have acuity in the range of 20/200 and 20/50. Acuity improves steadily thereafter and most children reach 20/20 by the age of ten or eleven. So while your newborn baby cannot see things that are very far away, and probably cannot see well enough to tell a tall object 10 feet (3m) away, she sees very well close up, and can focus her eyes at a distance of about 8 inches (20 cm), which is just about the usual distance between her eyes and your face during feeding. If your newborn baby can see you, you will almost certainly see a look of attention when your eyes make contact.

CAN YOUR BABY SEE YOU?

Here is a checklist of some of the general signs you can look for in your baby's first year.

Newborn

Newborn babies love looking at faces and they mainly look at the edge of the face or at the eyes, but they also look at things that move — like an adult's mouth. If you move your eyes and open and close your mouth in an exaggerated way, as you would when talking excitedly, your newborn baby will respond by moving his mouth and sticking out his tongue.

By 8 weeks

Your baby's brain has developed more fully and his attention shifts to what an object is, rather than where it is. So your baby's vision moves from a strategy of finding things to identifying things. How your baby should recognise your face and respond to it with smiles and jogging of the arms.

By 12 to 16 weeks

Your baby is now not only looking at the edges of things but taking in details, and she can notice whether two pictures are placed horizontally or vertically. Your baby can also tell the difference between pictures with two things in them and pictures with three things in them, and she now can clearly notice patterns.

By 20 to 24 weeks

Your baby can now see your face so well and take in such fine details that he can discriminate between different emotional expressions such as sadness, fear, or joy, and you will see the response in his face. He will get excited when he sees his feed being prepared.

From 24 weeks onwards

Your baby now starts to perceive that certain things are constant such as size, object type, object shape, and colour. She starts to identify objects and realises that an object is permanent, even if she does not see it. So, for instance, about now your child begins to understand that you continue to exist even when you have left the room. Now he will adjust his position to see objects that he is interested in.

By one year

Your baby can follow rapidly moving objects and see them quite clearly.

Up to three years

Your child can see and identify different letters of the alphabet and can match letters to those she has been given when asked to do so. She can do the same with toys.

VISION TESTS

NEWBORN

Procedure
With your fingers held eight to ten inches (20 to 25 cm) away from your baby's eyes move your fingers in front of your baby for about 12 inches (30 cm) on either side of his head.

Response
Your baby should follow your fingers for a distance of about six inches (15 cm) on either side of the mid-line.

FOUR WEEKS

Procedure
With your fingers held eight to ten inches (20 to 25 cm) away from your baby's eyes move your fingers in front of your baby for about 12 inches (30 cm) on either side of his head.

Response
Your baby should follow your fingers for a range of about eighteen inches to twenty four inches (45 to 60 cm).

12 WEEKS

Procedure
With your fingers held eight to ten inches (20 to 25 cm) away from your baby's eyes move your fingers in front of your baby for about 12 inches (30 cm) on either side of his head.

Response
He should be able to follow your fingers completely from one side to the other so that his eyes move in a range of 180 degrees.

Action
If your baby is unable to follow your fingers over this range of movement by the age of 12 weeks you should consult your doctor.

16 WEEKS

A new born baby's eyes tend to move independently but binocular vision (each eye follows the movement of the other eye so that your baby starts to see things in three dimensions), is present by 16 weeks.

Procedure
Show your baby a familiar object like a bottle or a toy that he might want to get hold of.

Response
When your baby's eyes are fixed you will see a response in his face: joy at seeing the bottle, or curiosity when he sees his toy.

Action
If your baby does not respond in this way to interesting sights consult your doctor.

20 WEEKS

Procedure
Check that your baby is now able to see his own hand by placing him on his back.

Response
Your baby will be intently watching the movements of his own fingers and try to put his hands together so that his fingers can touch.

24 WEEKS

Procedure
Check that your baby is responding to visual stimuli a little out of direct view by placing his toys to his side.

Response
Your baby will adjust his position in order to see objects, bending backwards or lowering his head in order to get a good view.

Action
If your baby does not behave in this way you should consult your doctor.

ONE YEAR

Procedure
To test response to movement, move an object fast across your baby's field of vision.

Response
Your baby should be able to follow a rapidly moving object with his eyes, without turning his head.

Action
If your baby doesn't follow a moving object consult your doctor.

TWO YEARS ONWARDS

Procedure using letter cards
Have two identical sets of the seven letters below. Give one to your child. Hold up a letter and ask your child to hold up one of his that is the same. After testing both eyes have your child cover one of his eyes at a time then repeat the test for each eye.

Response
The majority of three year olds can match the five simple letter shapes T, H, O, V and X at ten feet (3 m). A few two year olds can do this test but many confuse V and X. The majority of four year olds can match seven letters.

Procedure using small toys
To test distant vision, one of two sets of selected objects – car, plane and chair, a small doll, and a child's knife, fork, and spoon – should be given to your child. You walk to 10 feet (3 m) away and hold up each one asking your child to show his. Then repeat the test for each eye by having your child cover one and then the other. It helps if you hold up the objects against a black background. Near vision can be tested by asking your child to pick up small sweets, crumbs, pieces of thread, "pills" of cotton wool.

Response
Two year olds should be able to match the objects.

Action
If you detect any impairment of sight take your child to your doctor for a more detailed examination.

TESTING FOR SPECIAL PROBLEMS

PERIPHERAL VISION

Procedure
Play this particular test as a hide and seek game; using a favourite toy, have your child stare straight ahead and then slowly bring the toy alongside the side of his head and see if he sees it. Bring it further and further around in a semi-circle towards the mid-line and get him to indicate when he sees it.

Response
He should be able to see objects that are at an angle of 180 degrees.

COLOUR BLINDNESS
Procedure
Using coloured blocks, ask your child to select different colours. If he does not know his colours yet show him an example, and ask him to follow, choosing red when you choose red. From three years just request the colour.

Response
Your child should be able to pick the appropriate colours. If he persistently errs on the red or green, particularly if a boy, suspect colour blindness. This is most prevalent in boys. Red-green colour blindness is the most common; these become muddy shades of brown.

SQUINT
Procedure
Hold your baby so her head is central and have someone direct a light at her eyes. Now cover one eye at a time; notice whether the eye moves on uncovering it.

Response
The light reflex should be present in the same position in each eye. When uncovered, a squint-free eye will not move.

Action
Babies are normally tested for squint at six, nine and 12 months but you should consult your doctor or clinic if your baby shows a constant squint at any age.

LIGHT SENSITIVITY
Procedure
Expose your child's eyes momentarily to a bright light at frequent intervals.

Response
If she is light sensitive her eyes will tear a lot and give her discomfort. Consult your doctor.

TOOLS FOR LEARNING

TOOLS FOR LEARNING

The natural way for a child to learn is through play. For children, play and learning are not opposites; children benefit from "learning" situations that are enjoyable. Using building and construction toys, working with jigsaws, dominos, and threading toys, and matching colours, textures, and shapes, for example, children acquire essential skills, which later enable them to learn to read, write, and count.

Purpose-made toys are not strictly essential to learning, as children will invent their own games and toys anyway, but well-designed toys can provide stimuli for exploring and discovering new things. Nor need toys be expensive or complicated. The best toys are ones that fascinate a child, and to which she will return again and again. Often a household item, such as a washing up bowl that can be used for a boat, car, or pool, will provide hours of imaginative play. In fact, to provide your child with the kind of playthings she needs to ensure future intellectual achievement, it is not necessary to buy even one "educational" toy!

PROVIDING A STIMULATING ENVIRONMENT

One of the ways in which you can encourage your child's development is to foster creative play with an inviting environment. Simply the way you display your child's toys to a large extent determines whether they will be played with or not. When toys are piled higgledy-piggledy in a toy box, they are not inviting to a child, whereas well-displayed, orderly toys arranged into little scenes or little tableaux stimulate him to play, and to make other creative arrangements.

It helps if there are spaces to play in particular activity areas, like a sand tray, a painting table and somewhere your child can splash about with water. As long as you take proper safety precautions, the kitchen is an ideal place to play, especially if you have child-sized tables and chairs, a toy stove, some dishes, and even your pots and pans to play with. It is possible to arrange a dolls' corner where the dolls can be put to bed each evening, and got up in the morning for breakfast. Toys can be simple, cradles can be made of baskets lined with cloth, and a very small high chair and drawer for dolls' clothes adds to the realistic setting for a dolls' house.

An interesting environment should not be confined just to indoors. If you are fortunate enough to have a garden, you can fill it with suitable equipment such as a sand box, a swing, a slide, a climbing frame, a balancing board, a little hill make out of turf – all of which will stimulate your child's imagination.

CHOOSING TOYS

Anyone who has ever experienced it will empathise with the feeling of frustation encountered when, having spent hours choosing the safest, most colourful, most fun, most educational toy for their child, the ungrateful recipient, unaware of the stimulating possibilities being presented to him, clings steadfastly to his favourite saucepan lid. The lesson to be learned from this is that it is almost impossible to choose a "best toy" for your child. The one that is best is the one that fascinates him endlessly and to which he will return, gaining more and more stimulation and enjoyment. This may cost a lot, or cost nothing, but it is ultimately the toy that a child enjoys, which is going to provide him with the greatest learning experience.

Contrary to what parents expect, the less formed and more basic a toy, the more possibility it leaves for a child's imagination. So a piece of wood that can be used as a sword, wand, or baton, for example may help your child's creativity more than a very expensively dressed doll which can only be one character.

Having said this, there are some very well-designed toys which can provide your child with stimuli for exploring and discovering new things and for learning new skills. Below I've set out some criteria to help you to make the best choice of toy for your child.

Appropriateness to age

One of the most important things to remember is that children change very rapidly, particularly in the first three years, and that a toy which entertains a two-month-old will not entertain a two-year-old and vice-versa. As they develop, children need different stimuli and the choice of toys must reflect these differing needs. It is very important that the toy chosen for a child is appropriate to her age. If the toy is too advanced she will not know how to play with it in the proper way and will gain little enjoyment. If the toy is too primitive then she will become easily bored.

A very small child needs to have toys which will stimulate all five senses; suitable toys for a baby under one year are those which give experience of colours, textures, materials, and interesting and varied shapes. Toys which make noises and react to actions, such as rattles, give the child a sense of control, and encourage the development of manipulation skills and co-ordination.

Toddlers enjoy "putting in–taking out" games, so bricks of different sizes and shapes, plastic cups, spoons, bath toys, beakers, and round discs which fit on vertical pieces of wood and pyramids all prove popular. A most useful and enduring toy to buy at this stage is a sack of bricks of different sizes and shapes, which can be enjoyed now as put in–take out toys, but later will be used for great imaginative play such as building houses, boats and so on.

At about two years of age children aquire the skill of wrist-rotation which enables them to to unscrew things and open doors. Toys with lids that unscrew, interlocking bricks, more advanced shape sorters with differently-shaped blocks that will fit only one hole, formboards, and hammering benches, are all good developmental toys to give children at this stage.

The pre-school child continues to enjoy bricks, drawing and painting materials, and any object which stimulates imaginative play. He or she can begin to play simple games like snap or picture dominoes. All my children love to play games, and these are good for children because they encourage foresight and the ability to look ahead to see the consequence of an action. A game also gives them the opportunity to get one over on you. Bear in mind that all games are more educational to your children if you participate. Card games, for example, not only help to improve numerical ability, but also encourage the mastery of strategy. This quality is important in helping children to work towards targets. It encourages concentration, the ability to stick at a project and finish it, and speeds up their mental development.

Versatility and stimulation

Having decided upon the appropriate type of toys for your child's age range there are a few more things to be considered when purchasing them. First, is it completely safe? Second, is it stimulating? Third, does it have play value? In other words will the toy be versatile enough to be incorporated into many types of play and will it grow with your child? Fourth, very simply, is it fun? To make a very simple comparison, a sack of bricks is a "good" toy to buy because it can be enjoyed at different ages with equal pleasure, and will stimulate imaginative and active play. Mechanical toys are not so good because there is simply not much you can do with them and a child will become very bored quickly.

All of us know that toys can be educational, but toys can also enrich the kind of perceptions that your child experiences. By far the most useful toys in this respect are toys which allow your child to do

something to them, rather than force your child to play in a stereo-typed way. So, from an early age, toys that fit together or snap together, which can be used to build different constructions, also teach children that they can change the appearance of things with their own dexterity. In addition to this, they improve their spatial intelligence and depth of perception. Since boys are generally more gifted in these areas, toys of this kind are particularly good for girls.

If your child still prefers her saucepan lid, do not despair as household objects can make very good, fun, safe toys. Your child's reaction should be paramount in assessing whether or not you have chosen the best toy at any particular juncture. You do not have to buy the latest in educational toys as whatever your child is fascinated by is educational for her. Children are natural learners and anything in which a child has an interest is teaching her something.

Safety

Safety is obviously the most important consideration when choosing, or making a toy for your child. Whilst a few knocks, bruises and grazes are a natural and inevitable part of an adventurous child's play, there are ways in which you can ensure that you are giving your child a safe, fun toy to play with and not a potentially harmful weapon. The old joke "we bought her an unbreakable toy, so she broke all the others with it" rings very true to most parents who know how destructive children can be. Therefore, you must not only check toys for dangerous design faults when you are purchasing them, but also at regular intervals thereafter to make sure that none have developed. For example, have Teddy's firmly attached eyes worked loose with lots of pulling? Have plastic parts on toys broken leaving sharp edges? Toys designed for very small babies obviously have to be particularly carefully designed as babies do not have the dexterity to get themselves out of any difficulty, which may be caused by a toy.

Some specific points to check for on pram toys are:

- ☐ *Is the baby rattle light enough to prevent injury when your child inevitably hits himself with it?*

- ☐ *Do rattles or teethers have any parts long or slim enough to reach the back of your baby's throat?*

- ☐ *Are there any holes, small enough to trap your baby's fingers?*

- ☐ *Are there any long strings on the toy that can be swallowed or become wrapped around your baby's neck?*

When considering furry toys you should ensure that the toy is machine washable, and colour-fast; apart from the annoyance of having the colour sucked off, the dye could be harmful. The materials used should be flame retardant and the stuffing of a safe material that cannot be inhaled and choked upon. All hard features, such as eyes and noses, should be very firmly attached and not by spikes or pins.

Slightly older and more mobile children have a greater potential for destruction and natural inquisitiveness; small objects will be put into their mouths, noses and ears. A good rule of thumb for a toy is that no single part should have a dimension of less than one and a half inches. Before you buy make sure:

- ☐ *That toys are toughened so they cannot develop small or sharp parts through breakage;*

- ☐ *All paints, crayons and dough are non-toxic;*

- ☐ *Electrical toys have sufficiently large batteries; those with small calculator-size batteries should be avoided as they can be easily swallowed or pushed into ears or noses;*

- ☐ *Any electrical toys should present no danger of electrocution;*

- ☐ *Toys designed to take a child's weight, such as indoor wheelie toys, are strong and stable.*

Once a child is old enough to have large toys to play with in the garden a whole new set of hazards can arise. Outdoor gear and toys should be very carefully inspected, installed and checked for faults at regular intervals.

- ☐ *Install garden toys carefully on grass or another soft, flat surface – never on concrete;*

- ☐ *Slides, swings and other toys should be checked regularly for strength, stability and possible corrosion;*

- ☐ *Nothing on larger equipment should cause scissoring, shearing or pinching injuries;*

- ☐ *Make sure that all surfaces are smooth, in order to prevent snags or splinters;*

- ☐ *Material for tents, playhouses or tunnels is flame retardant;*

- ☐ *Cover a sandpit to prevent animals taking up residence or using it as a toilet;*

- ☐ *Never allow small children in paddling pools unsupervised as it is quite possible for them to drown in a couple of inches of water;*

- ☐ *Instruct children carefully on what they can and can't do on equipment.*

It is impossible to provide a child with a totally safe environment as children are naturally inquisitive and homes and gardens are not designed to be child proof. If, however, you take sensible safety precautions and can satisfy your child's inquisitiveness with safe indoor and outdoor toys, the risk of serious accident will be greatly reduced. Bear in mind, too, that young children should always be properly supervised and never left to play alone outdoors.

USING HOUSEHOLD ITEMS TO MAKE TOYS

You do not have to spend a lot of money to provide your child with the best (or better) toys than money can buy. A quick look around your own kitchen, and a bit of imagination on your and your child's part can provide your child with hours of fascinating fun.

Containers

Plastic food containers, yoghurt pots, ice cream tubs, plastic cups, washed out squeezy bottles, pans and strong tins, are perhaps the simplest, easiest, and the most versatile household toys. Plastic cartons of differing sizes can be used for hours of putting in–taking out games, scooping and pouring water at bathtime, sand in the sandpit, or transporting mud around the garden. Put a few pieces of pasta or dried peas inside a firmly closed container and you have a rattle or a musical instrument. Add a couple of wooden spoons and a whole drum set is invented – particularly effective with saucepans! Strong tins placed upside down in the garden can make stepping stones, or if you make holes in them and tie long pieces of string to their tops, you produce safe stilts, that will help improve balance. For a younger child, yoghurt pots hung from a plastic hanger will make a very effective mobile.

Food

Pasta, beans and other dried goods make very good toys. They can all be used as the noisy element inside a toy, can be stuck to pieces of card to make kitchen collages, and can be painted and threaded onto string or elastic to make jewellery (see overleaf). Make sure you keep your child under supervision as dried peas and beans can be inhaled or prodded into bodily orifices.

Vegetables such as potatoes, leeks, and carrots can be made into printing blocks (see overleaf); leeks make good spirals just left alone. Most children enjoy being given a bit of pastry to shape for themselves to be cooked in with the 'proper' food.

Paper goods

Cardboard tubes such as those in toilet rolls or kitchen roll, given a little decoration will make finger puppets. Hand puppets can be made of paper bags. Cardboard egg boxes, decorated inside and out, make great monsters as the hinge of the box will open and shut like a jaw.

Empty cotton reels threaded onto a length of string will make a good pull toy, especially if painted to look like a caterpillar or snake.

HOME-MADE FUN

Baker's clay

Mix together 225g cornstarch and 350g baking soda in a large pot. Add 360ml water at once, and stir until thickened and smooth. Turn onto a cool, heatsafe surface, and cover with a damp cloth. Once the dough has cooled, knead it with hands coated with cornstarch until it is smooth and pliable. You could divide it into smaller balls and knead in food colouring to make brightly coloured dough. Roll out and cut out shapes using cookie cutters, or cut freehand around shapes. To dry, place the cut-out shaped dough on a baking sheet and bake at 250°C to 300°C until hard.

Soap bubbles and blower

Dilute 180ml liquid dishwashing detergent or tearless shampoo with 1.8 litres water. Add 240ml glycerine to make the bubbles stronger. Make a simple blower by twisting one end of a pipe cleaner into a ring.

Modelling dough

Mix 625g plain flour, 300g salt and
5 tablespoons salad oil in a large
bowl. Add 240–480ml water a little
at a time. If the dough becomes
sticky, add more flour; it should be
dry and handle easily. To colour
the dough, divide into balls and
put on a few drops of food colour
into a depression made in each
ball. Squeeze and roll the ball on a
floured, washable surface to mix
the colour. If the dough gets sticky,
add more flour. To make a scented
dough, add some fruit-flavoured
gelatin powder. Store the dough in
a plastic bag in a refrigerator
for up to three weeks.

Finger paint

Dissolve 125g laundry starch or 225g cornstarch
in a little cold water. Add 900ml boiling water
and bring the mixture back to the boil. Cook
until thick. Remove the mixture from the heat
and stir in 40g pure white soap flakes or
powder. Divide the mixture into small
containers and colour with poster paint, water
crayons, or food colouring. Almost any
household object can be used to make
interesting prints and patterns. For example,
combs, pegs, sponge, cotton reels, cardboard
tubes. Plastic egg boxes and old bun baking
trays make good palettes for the aspiring
painter.

Pasta jewellery

Spray pasta bows with two or more colours of spray paint and allow to dry. Thread onto a piece of shirring elastic to make a pretty pasta necklace or bracelet.

Vegetable printers

Using a small, very sharp knife incise a simple pattern, such as a triangle or star, in a carrot or a potato. Then, cut from the side and gently lever out the unwanted parts, leaving the pattern raised. Make as many shapes as you like, using a different vegetable for each and dip into paint to make colourful repeating prints and patterns.

Rainy day beach

Fill a large cake tin or washing up bowl with cornmeal or aquarium gravel. Place in the middle of a large beach towel or old sheet and add lots of containers and spoons for digging.

Rainy day waves

Add safe detergent and an egg whisk to a large bowl of water. With a few good beats lovely frothy waves will appear.

Glue

Bring 180ml water, 2 tablespoons corn syrup and 1 teaspoon white vinegar to a rolling boil. In a separate bowl, mix together 125g cornstarch with the rest of the water. While constantly stirring, slowly add the cornstarch mixture to the hot mixture. Let the glue stand overnight before using.

Foil decorations

Scrunch foil into "jewels", or use as bodies for models. Cut into strips with pinking shears, and stick to make gleaming party paper chains. Draw a series of triangles down from the edge of a stiff piece of gold card. Cut these out carefully to make a crown. Wrap a toilet roll tube with some shiny paper, add some imaginative curls, or some stick-on paper jewels and you can make a glittering party table decoration.

"Edible" finger paint for babies

Mix 75g rye or plain wheat flour and water in a saucepan. Stirring constantly, bring to simmering point. Add the cornstarch mixed with 4 tablespoons cold water. Allow the paint to cool and colour with small amounts of food colouring or bits or water crayons.

Baby play dough

In a large bowl, mix 425g flour, 120ml salad oil and 120ml water. Knead well, adding more water if necessary to bind the mixture together. If you like, colour with food colouring.

THE COMPUTER

As children many of us had blind spots in our learning. Some of us had difficulty with writing essays, others with mathematics. The computer is a most marvellous device for showing mathematical relationships and the hand-held "joy-stick" on computer games is an ideal bridge for your child, between play and learning about the building blocks of mathematics. It is also a way for children to get immediately the point of what they are doing, because they can fit the actions of their hands to a result on the screen. In this way they start to learn about the joy of feedback. It teaches an approach to planning and problem solving that will quickly extend to other areas of learning and everyday activities. However, computers are best bought for older children; they aren't really suitable for pre-school children who lack the competence to master them.

TELEVISION AND VIDEO

Television can be very educational, with children's programmes helping to teach children how to read, count, and introducing them to imaginative ideas and experiences. However, while the old "children's hour" used to provide just about the right length of exposure to the television, technological advances, such as more channels, cable television, and particularly videos, have made it possible for children to sit glued to a television set all day.

Far from being stimulating, the television has a mesmerising and numbing effect on children as it cuts them off from the direct experience of their world which they need in order to develop. Every parent knows that the television will quieten noisy children, and often children will sit very close to the television in order to blot out any external distractions. It can be very tempting for parents to use the television to distract their children when they don't have time or energy to concentrate upon playing. This unfortunately cuts down the amount of social contact with the parent which is so important for social and linguistic development. Story-time which ideally involves the parent and child following through a book together, and the child using his imagination and beginning to recognise written words, may become replaced by video-time in which the child is isolated and is the recipient of information about his world which he might have more fun discovering himself.

Even thinking parents today may justify the time they "buy" in letting their children watch television by kidding themselves that they only let their children watch special children's programmes or educational programmes. A new way of looking at the time your children spend watching television is what they are not able to do while they are glued to the television set.

TELEVISION PREVENTS YOUR CHILD:

- [ ] *Scanning, sifting and analysing information and then applying it to everyday situations*
- [ ] *Practising motor skills, be they gross or fine*
- [ ] *Practising coordination of eye and hand*
- [ ] *Using more than two senses at a time to expand the appreciation of his or her environment*
- [ ] *Asking questions and receiving helpful educational answers*
- [ ] *Exploring and using his or her curiosity*
- [ ] *Exercising initiative or motivation*
- [ ] *Being challenged*
- [ ] *Solving problems*
- [ ] *Thinking analytically*
- [ ] *Using his or her imagination*
- [ ] *Practising communication skills*
- [ ] *Improving verbal skills*
- [ ] *Writing and reading*
- [ ] *Being either creative or constructive*
- [ ] *Not promoting the ability to concentrate for long periods because of the television's flicker*
- [ ] *Not promoting logical, sequential thinking because the action shifts constantly backwards and forwards and laterally in time*

Parents may argue that television can stimulate imagination, as children will often act out their favourite television characters. Certainly we all have or had characters which we loved to imitate as children but, if stimulated in more active ways, such as dressing-up, children are brilliant at inventing their own characters. Television produces a kind of imaginative laziness as it performs the function of imaginative invention.

Some television can be a valuable experience for your child as she can learn new concepts, such as telling the time, and have fun doing so. It is another source of information for your child. However, experts agree that about one hour of television per day is enough for a small child. Otherwise, the time that should be spent in active play, discovering and communicating, is lost and could limit your child's full-blown development.

BOOKS AND READING

If I had to choose a single way in which a parent could enrich his or her child's environment and help her to develop well, I would suggest having books in the house. If you enjoy reading, make it obvious and talk about it, your child will too. Words are crucial to the way our brains function, reading is therefore very important and there is a correlation between how many books you have in the house and how much your child will read as she grows up and later in life.

Books are one of the great pleasures of life, and are vital in providing your child with the words to express feelings, ideas and thoughts. Moreover, they explain the world he or she lives in –

describing relationships, depicting situations and introducing person-alities. Books provide the impetus for imaginative play, they intro-duce ideas, and they are fun.

Youngsters always copy their parents. So if you read books, your child will too. Of course, in the beginning, it helps if reading experience is shared. In our house, books were introduced to our children before the end of the first year, usually around nine or ten months and it was always a shared experience. It might last only a few minutes if the child was not particularly interested but we "read" several times a day.

Encouraging your child to read

You are more certain to create in your child a desire to read if he finds reading books a successful and enjoyable experience. Try to read to your child every day, or at the minimum, several times a week, and get in the habit of reading to him at the same time.

Choose books of the appropriate interest level for your child, that are visually appealing with good illustrations. Children like pictures and photographs of people, places, and events with which they are familiar. They also like pictures of animals. Fairy tales are fascinating to children. Theory says they can be useful tools for a child to learn painlessly about the world, and to make a distinction between the real and the unreal. Fairy tales encourage abstract thought and creative thinking.

First reading books should be short with only a few pages as the attention span of a young child is short. They should also have large illustrations with few details. Many children like books that contain illustrations and no words.

Make certain the vocabulary is easy to understand. A book with big print may look easy but can contain difficult words, so read it through first to see if the words will be comprehensible to your child.

When reading to your child he or she will enjoy it more if the atmosphere is relaxed and cosy.

As you read, run your finger along under the print but don't force your child to look at the words or follow your finger.

Encourage your child to notice things in the pictures or make guesses at what will happen next; give praise when she does so.

If your child asks, re-read books; a favourite book may be read many, many times. The best way to gauge whether your child is interested in a subject is how much he talks about it and how often he goes back to read his favourite book spontaneously.

When your child indicates that he is ready to read, offer familiar, favourite books that can be "read" even though your child has memorized the words. At a later stage, your child will see these familiar words in other books and be able to read them then.

Provide your child with new books that tell a story with a lot of repetition and have the same words appearing over and over.

Don't stop reading to your child even though she is reading by herself. Your child will still continue to enjoy the luxury of having you spend time with her in this intimate way.

Teach your child to take care of books, to keep them clean, in good condition, and free of scribbles.

Store books on low bookshelves in your child's room; this will invite browsing. Make sure always to have a variety on hand.

PARENTAL-LED ACTIVITIES

As your child's first teacher there is a lot which it is better that you do not do. Stimulate your child by all means but do not over stimulate her or force her beyond her readiness. Do not push your child into academic tasks before she is ready for them; take your lead from her.

Lessons, workbooks, academic tasks, even flash cards, are used prematurely by many parents before the imaginative world of early childhood has time to flower. The natural time for these educational aids is from six or seven onwards, and not before, otherwise you will rob your child of the valuable years of early childhood, which are so vital to physical health and mental development. Trying to speed up the development of your child when he is very young places him at risk, and there is no apparent gain to justify this risk.

In all exercises, it is important to be enthusiastic, supportive, uncritical and praise and reward your child with some kind of treat. You might, for instance, be discriminating about letting your child watch a television programme, or a cassette of a good film suitable for children. If you possibly can, sit with your child and discuss what is going on on the screen so there is some sort of dialogue and thought while your child is watching. Of course, the best reward of all is being in your company.

Language exercises

The English language is extremely rich in that its vocabulary can give many shades of meaning. Even individual words can have many subtle nuances, and your child will gradually master these shades of grey. You can help your child by showing an interest in words and the way you use them and how useful they are, for example, just take the colour red and think how many similar words there are to describe redness e.g. heat, fire, crimson, scarlet, postbox, maroon, fire-engine, pink, poppy, apple, etc. Just run your child through a list like this to expand her collection of words.

A child can understand the concept of opposite from a very early age such as cold/hot, big/small, nice/nasty. To move on from there you can introduce more complex judgements like words that describe the states of mind between joyousness and sadness; e.g. excited, elated, happy, content, tranquil, serene, quiet, moody, off colour, depressed etc.

A good way of increasing your child's vocabulary and the way to describe her feelings is to let her choose one of her favourite objects and describe what it would be like if she were that object. You might choose a bell and ask your child what she felt like. She might say "I love ringing"; then you can ask what kind of ring it is, is it a high pitched ring or a deep clunk? and then, because they are made of metal, does she feel hot or cold? does she shine? does she like being picked up and rung?

Children start asking questions before the age of three so you should start asking them questions around the same time. Initially, of course, the questions are very simple "How does that toy work?" but later your questions can be much more searching and relate to your child's experience. "Can you think of an example of that?", "What does that mean to you?". The crucial element here is that you should listen to the answers, not state whether the answer is right or wrong but use your child's answer to move on to another question and enlarge the discussion.

All my children loved treasure hunts, particularly trying to work out what the various clues meant, and this is a very subtle way of familiarising your child with language "codes", abbreviations, meanings behind the words, reading between the lines. As your children grow older, you can make the codes more complicated such as taking a simple rhyme and underlining the letters that make the words of the message. All of these things help your child to see language, reading, writing and using words as a game more than labour. Your child can then go on to make her own codes which she can break with her friends helping.

Games are an ideal way to acquire information on many levels. In our house we always had our own set of house-rules for certain games like Scrabble and Monopoly, and it is a very good exercise for your children to help them "break the rules". As a first step in order to break the rules you have to understand them intimately. Then children have to learn sooner or later that rules are for interpretation not always for strict adherence, and this helps your child to see what positions in life are negotiable, and where there is room for manoeuvre. If, for instance, you decide that in Scrabble you will allow proper names that have been incorporated into the language like hoover, oxo, but not names beginning in capital letters, your child starts to make very subtle distinctions and therefore will understand more clearly what is allowable or not allowable in everyday life as well as learning about words.

Imagination exercises

From infancy you have been giving your child's imagination full rein but there are certain things that you can do that will encourage him to use his imagination even when you are not there to stimulate him. One of the best things you can teach your child is painting and drawing and the use of colour, but also modelling with clay or wax. Wax is particularly good because it is coloured, smells nice, is not messy, can be used over and over again, and seems to be alive because it models more easily as it gets warm. Just give your child a bit of coloured beeswax and suggest that he warms it in his hands; the changing shape in itself will stimulate his imagination to start modelling it. Warm a piece of wax in your hands at the same time as your child and start telling a story, a story no matter simple will give you both an idea of what to make, and you may ask for your child's idea, and then share yours and decide what you would like to make together. Make sure that you finish last so that you can give your child's creative instincts full rein. You can use beeswax from a very early age, because young children simply enjoy the texture, pinching it, and stretching it, and it has enormous possibilities for fantasy.

A little later, you can have your child make her own toys. All this not only encourages creativity but dexterity, a love of beautiful things, and judgement. There are all kinds of objects that your child can make, particularly if you are interested in certain activities. Show her how to sew, embroider, knit, crochet, string beads, make dolls, make presents for friends, simple things like handkerchiefs or place mats; boys can do these things as well as girls.

There are many natural materials that you can find on your outdoor trips. Collect bark, beautifully shaped branches, slices of logs, bird feathers, interestingly shaped leaves and make pictures, collages and patterns when you come home. Of course, you can always buy craft and design toys from shops to make objects, but to my mind, your child's imagination is given greater freedom if you allow the child to choose the materials to start with.

*Drawing
exercises*

It will help enormously if your child can make patterns out of the things that happen in life, both visual patterns, memory patterns, planning and strategy patterns, and you can encourage this thinking habit from a very early age by the use of simple jigsaws. Ask your child to make a drawing on a piece of paper, and then ask her to cut it into the smallest number of parts to make up the pattern again i.e. two parts, and then the largest number of parts. A similar exercise would be to buy fuzzy felt shapes and ask your child to create a picture or a pattern. As your child gets older, you can do more detailed drawings and cut them into more shapes as are found in complicated jigsaws.

You can help your child to become in touch with his feelings and to recognise feelings in others, by getting him to draw happy faces and sad faces, first with a guiding hand from you. Then move your child onto looking at photographs of people he knows and deciding how they are feeling in the photograph. This not only helps your child to recognise emotions but to empathise, and to relate closely to them. Later, you can take your child onto newspapers and magazines. Even at eighteen months my children loved looking at colour magazines naming objects, and pointing to objects that were named, but later looking at faces with me and deciding "What do you think that person is feeling?" or "What feeling is on this face?". Then perhaps I'd suggest what we might do to join in or soothe.

When your child is a little older, you can draw stick figures for your child and ask what the various postures mean in terms of feelings. Later, you can get your child to draw stick figures and to express the various emotions that they feel.

You can also use drawings to expand your child's view of the world. A very simple idea would be what happens when you spill water and you and your child could do a drawing of knocking over a jug of water and it spilling onto the floor and making a puddle, perhaps running off the edge of the table onto the floor in big drops and splashes. This

kind of exercise reinforces your child's memory and provides him with his own experience.

Whenever you are telling or writing a story, or when your child is old enough to do either of these things, always ask if there is any part of the story that could be illustrated and at first help your child and then get your child to draw some kind of picture, so that she can visualize what is in her imagination and express it in pictures, not only words. Even in conversation you can introduce the idea of mind pictures and get your child to describe the picture in her mind's eye, in words, not just in drawings.

Dressing up

Dressing up is one of the best ways to enhance your child's imagination. By doing so, your child can become another person or creature, and discover how it feels to be someone or something else. In this way, too, your child can play at controlling situations in which he would, in "real life", be powerless, and even to come to terms with fears and worries – all of which contributes to building confidence.

It is easy to keep a dressing up box with several items of your old clothes, hats, jewellery and shoes. Children can have hours of sheer fun putting on and taking off fancy clothes, and then acting out roles in imaginative play, especially if you invite friends of a similar age to come and play with them. On the practical side, make sure dressing-up clothes are simple to put on, do not trail on the floor, and do not have long cords fastening the neck.

Most children find that accessories are more important than costumes, and a few items are enough to evoke a scenario. You can make a crown out of stiff paper and cover it with aluminium foil, and you can take a couple of squares of thin material like chiffon and they can be worn as veils. You also can make a collection of uniform hats such as sailor, farmer, policeman, train driver.

TOYS FOR BABIES NEWBORN TO 6 MONTHS

The young baby is not capable of much manipulation so he is seeking to experience the world very much through sight, sound and touch. He likes looking at faces close up, and prefers objects that move, are brightly coloured and noisy. Create an appropriate environment by choosing cot sheets that have vivid patterns, and dressing him in socks that have bright designs or faces.

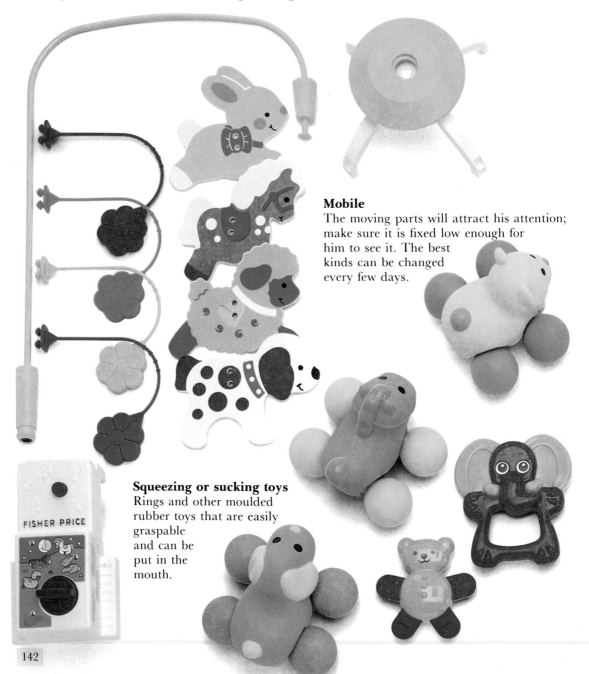

Mobile
The moving parts will attract his attention; make sure it is fixed low enough for him to see it. The best kinds can be changed every few days.

Squeezing or sucking toys
Rings and other moulded rubber toys that are easily graspable and can be put in the mouth.

FISHER PRICE

142

Soft toys or balls
The most desirable
are simply constructed
of varying textures.

**Plastic-coated photographs
and baby mirror**
These should be hung at
side of crib where baby
can see them.

Rattle, bells, squeaker
Toys that make noise when thrown,
batted, squeezed, sucked or shaken.

ACTIVITIES AND GAMES FOR BABIES NEWBORN TO 6 MONTHS

Sound and Word Activities	Sing to your baby: croon lullabies while nursing, cuddling or rocking your baby to sleep.	
Physical Activities and Games	Dance with your baby: rock, croon to, and sway back and forth to the beat of some simple, melodic tunes. Simple games babies enjoy include baby sit-ups, knee rides, and galloping around the room done gently and always with the baby well supported.	

TOYS FOR BABIES 7 TO 12 MONTHS

The older baby can remember simple concepts and identify herself, her body parts, and people familiar to her. She is fascinated by items and will explore them, putting them in and out of containers, and searching for them if they are hidden. She will be imitating sounds and progressing towards walking. Offer her any of her earlier toys plus the following:

Free-standing rattles
Can be set on feeding tables and near baby's seat to encourage swipes.

Heavy cardboard, cloth or vinyl books
These should have large, simple illustrations, and be made of material that can be grasped, shaken and chewed.

Balls
Ones of all different sizes, both hard and soft, are suitable.

Movable toys
Cars, buses or animals that move on rubber or large plastic wheels.

Large soft blocks
Can be used for building
as well as squeezing
and throwing.

Stuffed animals
These should be firmly
constructed and contain
no removable parts.

Beakers, cups, and floating toys
These can be used in the bath
and for other water play.

ACTIVITIES AND GAMES FOR BABIES 7 TO 12 MONTHS

Sound and Word Activities		Including blowing into empty paper rolls, imitating animal sounds, and singing songs such as *Old MacDonald Had A Farm* and *Pat-A-Cake*.
Physical Activities and Games		More active games such as piggy back rides and leg lifts are enjoyable for most older babies. Ball rolling can be started. Hiding games, such as *Peek-A-Boo* and *Which Hand* (hide an object in your hand so it can be easily found, and let her choose the correct one; praise her when she guesses right) will appeal to her sense of curiosity.
Indoor/ outdoor Play		Banging a pot and lid, hitting wooden spoons (these can be taped to reduce noise) against the bottom of a pot; sifting small amounts of flour; filling empty canisters, cans and boxes with wooden clothespins or blocks, is fun to do and provides lessons in sound making.

145

TOYS FOR TODDLERS 12 TO 18 MONTHS

Having mastered walking, a child of this age will like to follow you around imitating what you do. And, having achieved some measure of dexterity, he is most happy experimenting with items that challenge his manipulatory abilities. Now, too, that he speaks and understands some words and ideas, he will enjoy listening to stories.

Books
Those with different textures – touch and feel – as well as picture books with bright coloured illustrations are best.

Musical box or toys
Ones that jingle when moved will provide the most interest.

Puzzles
Should have knobs to make pieces easy to pick up, or a few very large pieces that are simple to put together.

Vehicles
These should be of a more sophisticated shape and made of wood or rubber.

Colouring materials
These will satisfy your child's need for scribbling.

Stacking toys
Rings and blocks
encourage dexterity and
spatial visualisation.

Push and pull toys
Ones with strings to pull
or with rigid handles,
and carts to load and
unload are particularly
recommended.

Nesting toys
These can be
built up as
well as fitted
together; the
larger sized
ones can be used
as containers for
large beads, etc.

ACTIVITIES AND GAMES FOR TODDLERS 12 TO 18 MONTHS

🎵	**Sound and Word Activities**	Continue singing nursery rhymes, which are excellent for language development and talk to your child as often as possible, using adult speech, not "baby talk."
🎲	**Physical Activities and Games**	Simple movement games like *Ring-A-Rosy*, *Clap Hands*, *Follow the Leader*, and *Hide and Seek* (make certain you are not too hard to find!) are good to work off some of your baby's excess energy.
🖌️	**Artistic Activities**	Pasting, colouring and painting can be done under supervision. Make certain all materials are non-toxic or use some of the recipes set out on pages 130–133.
🏠	**Indoor/ outdoor Play**	Sand boxes and water trays can provide hours of fun. Provide your child with household containers and measuring cups, home-made bubbles (see p.130–133), or commercially available toys.

TOYS FOR TODDLERS 18 MONTHS TO 2 YEARS

The child of up to two years does not like to share although she usually likes to play with others. She spends a longer time playing by herself with toys that she can manage independently, particularly those that imitate the actions of grown-ups.

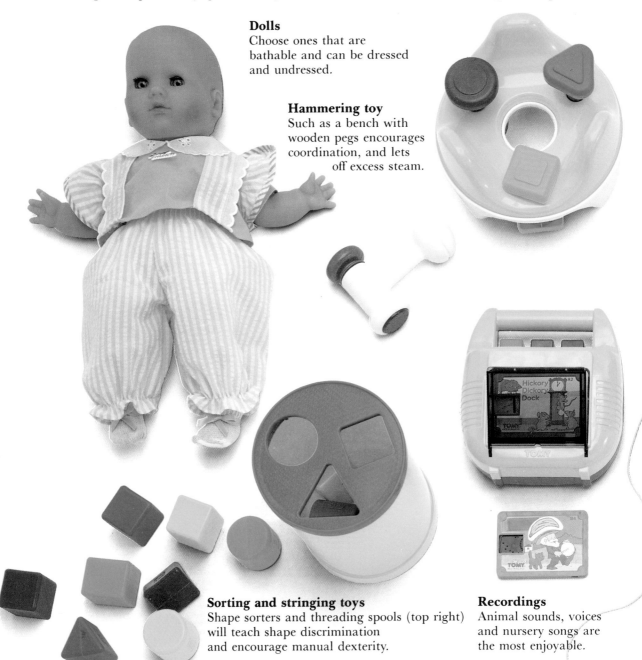

Dolls
Choose ones that are bathable and can be dressed and undressed.

Hammering toy
Such as a bench with wooden pegs encourages coordination, and lets off excess steam.

Sorting and stringing toys
Shape sorters and threading spools (top right) will teach shape discrimination and encourage manual dexterity.

Recordings
Animal sounds, voices and nursery songs are the most enjoyable.

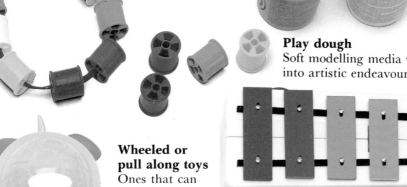

Play dough
Soft modelling media will introduce variety into artistic endeavours (see recipes p.130–133).

Wheeled or pull along toys
Ones that can be used indoors and out are the best choice.

Toy telephone
This will feed the need for conversation and other word play.

Musical toys
Simple ones can be used to accompany nursery songs or played for their own effects.

ACTIVITIES AND GAMES FOR TODDLERS 18 MONTHS TO 2 YEARS

Sound and Word Activities	Read aloud books with more words and especially those that rhyme; make up stories with your child as the heroine.	
Physical Activities and Games	Play and songs with actions: *Hokey Cokey* and *London Bridge is Falling Down* are entertaining, and can be played with other children.	
Artistic Activities	Glue collages using paper, polystyrene, string, rice, fabric, and other materials; finger painting and simple modelling will all challenge her. Make certain she does them under supervision.	

TOYS FOR CHILDREN 2 TO 3½

A child of this age gains steadily in independence, control of language, and new skills. He needs careful watching, though, as his sense of caution is not fully developed. He likes to build up items and knock them down, and put things together and take them apart; he will enjoy all things that test his abilities.

Tempera or water colour paints and scissors
Finer work can be attempted now. Offer only a few colours at a time and make certain scissors are blunt edged.

Construction toys of all types
These provide hours of entertainment.

Dressing up clothes
These encourage imagination along with "let's pretend" games.

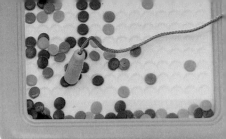

Manipulatory toys
Ones that require
fine movements can
be attempted now.

Simple games and large-piece puzzles
Choose ones with famliar subjects that can
be played alone or worked together.

**Tools and
household items**
Allow your child
to get on with work
at the same time
as you do.

ACTIVITIES AND GAMES FOR CHILDREN 2 TO 3½

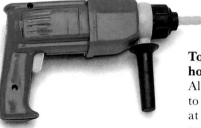

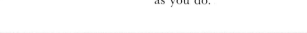

♪♫♩	**Sound and Word Activities**	Try alphabet games and counting ones, and introduce simple tongue twisters and jokes.
	Physical Activities and Games	Activities and games that revolve around music, such as *Musical Chairs* or *Pass the Parcel*, or those involving imitation, such as *Simple Simon*, are now within your child's abilities.
	Artistic Activities	Now is the time to introduce spatter painting, crayon rubbings and string painting to art work. Your child also can do potato prints and make simple stamps from carrots and cut-up sponges.
	Indoor/ outdoor Play	Simple cooking projects like having your child measure out ingredients, cut out cookies and shapes from sandwiches, make celery boats filled with a cheese spread, garnish food with slices of banana or cucumber, or getting him to set the table should be greeted with enthusiasm. *Nature activities* such as discussing sunrises, sunsets, rainbows, and stars, collecting leaves and flowers, sowing seeds or growing cuttings, should help your child understand his world.
	Visits	Trips to the library should now be started. Let your child choose books with simple stories and large-scale illustrations.

TOYS FOR CHILDREN 3½ TO 5

Playing together and sharing activities with other children are important now, and your child will exhibit a real curiosity about many things. She will be asking lots of questions and wanting to test her physical skills. She has an attention span long enough so that she can occupy herself for quite a while with various activities.

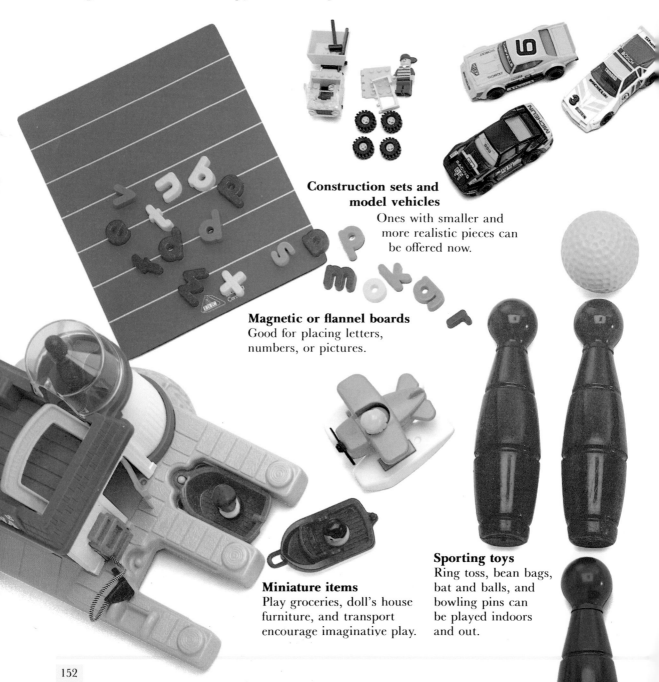

**Construction sets and
model vehicles**
Ones with smaller and
more realistic pieces can
be offered now.

Magnetic or flannel boards
Good for placing letters,
numbers, or pictures.

Miniature items
Play groceries, doll's house
furniture, and transport
encourage imaginative play.

Sporting toys
Ring toss, bean bags,
bat and balls, and
bowling pins can
be played indoors
and out.

Books

Pop-up and more complicated reading books and fill-in work and study books on writing and arithmetic, also simple science subjects are good choices.

Record or tape player

This should be sturdy and used to play a selection of your child's favourite songs or stories.

Magnifying glass and binoculars

These and other simple scientific instruments will give a child insight into another world.

ACTIVITIES AND GAMES FOR CHILDREN 3½ TO 5

	Sound and Word Activities	Concentrate on number rhymes and counting songs as a form of pre-school mathematics play.
	Games	Board games of a simple variety involving spinning a wheel, shooting dice or moving pieces will be enjoyed by the child now, as will be card games such as *Old Maid* and *Snap*.
	Artistic Activities	Making simple masks and hand puppets out of paper bags, tights and fabric is something children of this age can accomplish. Create "furniture," "vehicles" and "play houses" out of cardboard boxes and cartons, tubes and sheets.
	Visits	You can begin to take your child to the cinema, theatre and museums featuring shows for children; these will prove exciting now that your child is able to appreciate what he sees. Visits to zoos and animal parks can be turned into learning experiences if you prepare your child beforehand for what he will see.

TOYS FOR CHILDREN 5 TO 7

The school-age child shows an increasing interest in reading, writing and simple sums. She also is curious about the world and the way it works, and likes to engage in "grown-up" activities. She also is interested more in social activities, and likes to plan things to do with a friend.

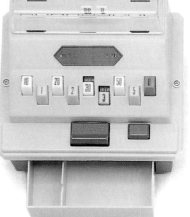

Dress-up dolls
Those with a variety of clothes and accessories provide hours of play.

Simple camera and film
These can be used to record holiday times as well as everyday activities.

Scaled-down versions of adult machines
Cash registers, typewriters and computers assist in pretend play.

Simple craft kits
Pressing flowers, knitting, weaving, card making or printing will be enjoyed by a child of this age.

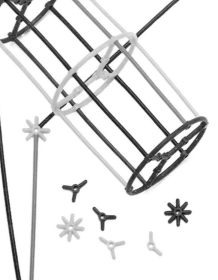

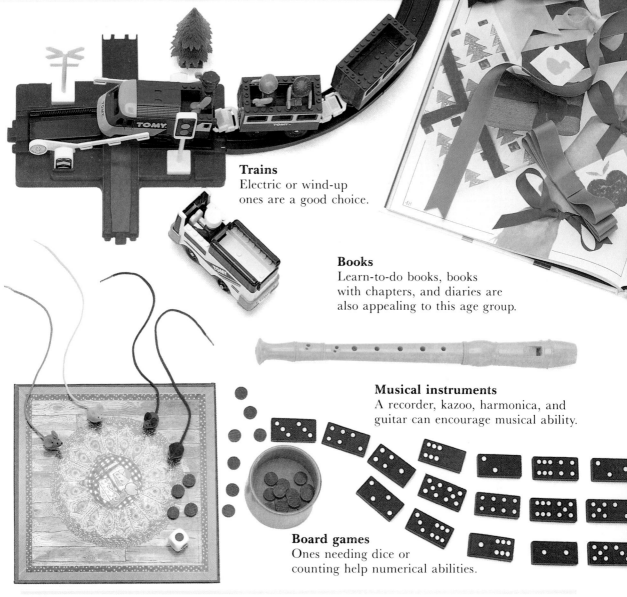

Trains
Electric or wind-up
ones are a good choice.

Books
Learn-to-do books, books
with chapters, and diaries are
also appealing to this age group.

Musical instruments
A recorder, kazoo, harmonica, and
guitar can encourage musical ability.

Board games
Ones needing dice or
counting help numerical abilities.

ACTIVITIES AND GAMES FOR CHILDREN 5 TO 7

	Artistic Activities	These now can include more advanced work such as making scrapbooks or starting a collection of stamps or coins, etc.
	Indoor/ outdoor Play	Nature activities should include collecting specimens of leaves, flowers, etc., and using dried flowers in artistic creations such as collages. "Pretend" play such as supplying your child with a "mini" office containing a stapler, hole punch, paper, pens, paper clips, and folders will let a child imitate "grown-up" work; a play shop is easy to stock with goods, packaging and money.

THE
SPECIAL
CHILD

THE SPECIAL CHILD

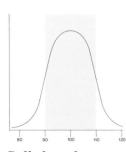

Bell-shaped curve
At the right-hand side of the curve is the small group of very gifted children who are achievers or even super achievers; at the left-hand side there is another small group of children whose mental abilities are impaired. The overwhelming majority of children fall in the middle.

A special child, one who needs particular care and attention, may be one who falls into either end of the mental abilities spectrum (see curve left), or whose development suffers from a learning disability, a physical impairment, or other handicap. All such children are particularly hard to parent, and all will require a special team effort from the whole family.

A gifted child can be just as difficult to parent as the child who has other special needs. Especially bright children can outstrip their parents and make them feel inadequate and somewhat helpless in trying to provide a stimulating environment in which they can grow. They can become bored and troublesome in ordinary lessons and, if misunderstood by adults and other children, can become antisocial and withdrawn.

A child with special needs is highly demanding of attention, love, and patience, which can be exhausting and sometimes soul destroying, especially if the child is capable only of making limited progress. However, with professional advice, parents can help such a child to reach his or her full potential – a highly rewarding experience for both parents and child.

A good, friendly and sympathetic doctor will be your best ally. He or she should be able to advise you about, or put you in touch with, medical specialists, educational associations, support groups, national associations, and charities, who are well-versed in your child's particular needs.

Parenting a special child is very demanding, and you must not expect yourself to be super-human and become a perfect parent for a difficult child immediately. Keeping yourself healthy and happy is as important as meeting your child's needs, and creating a successful family environment.

THE GIFTED CHILD

At some point in your child's development you are bound to think that she is gifted. Most children at some time are ahead of their age in one form of development or another, but super performance in one or two areas does not make your child especially bright. The characteristic of a bright child is that she is ahead of her age in nearly all forms of achievement and in the acquisition of skills. She is, across the board, a super-achieving child.

If you think your child is especially bright it could be a good idea to fill out the following questionnaire drawn up by Dr. David Weeks, which looks at a great number of traits, behaviours, preferences, and

QUESTIONNAIRE FOR DISCOVERING GIFTEDNESS IN YOUR CHILD

Procedure and scoring

Answer all questions. No answer is wrong and no answer is right. Give the first spontaneous answer as it comes into your head. In order to score your child you give 0 for never or not applicable, 3 for sometimes or applies somewhat, and 6 for always or applies absolutely.

Total ☐

0 never/not applicable	**3** sometimes/somewhat	**6** always/absolutely

☐ My child has seemed over-active but this has turned out to be far from aimless

☐ My child can understand ideas that are difficult for other children of his/her age

☐ My child has a purpose in finding out more about the world as he/she sees it

☐ My child obviously obtains enjoyment from day-dreaming

☐ My child revels in being that bit different

☐ My child feels that people ought to be more concerned about other people

☐ My child is never timid but quite outgoing with adults, in fact I suspect he/she prefers adults to children

☐ My child is talkative

☐ When asked particularly NOT to do something, my child often does just that anyway

☐ Other children could be jealous of my child's abilities

☐ My child has strong leanings toward academic activity

☐ My child becomes impatient because he/she wants to learn new things

☐ My child likes to solve puzzles that other children find difficult

☐ My child's vocabulary is unusual for a child of his/her age

☐ Being on his/her own does not worry my child in the slightest

☐ My child likes to find out what famous men and women have thought about various topics

☐ My child is extremely curious

☐ I would describe my child as being independent-minded

☐ My child is more sensitive than most to the environment around him/her

☐ My child does much more than what is expected of him/her

☐ My child appears to be free from anxieties and minor fears

☐ My child has already felt free to voice unpopular opinions

☐ In some respects, my child has not been happy at school

☐ My child loves to take things apart to find out how they work

☐ My child began drawing or reading early, and still enjoys these pursuits

☐ I would say that my child uses his/her solitude constructively

☐ My child seemed to grasp abstract ideas early on

☐ My child's mind appears to be very quick on the uptake

☐ My child has described his/her dreams to me without hesitating

☐ My child spends long periods of time studying without being asked to do so

attitudes, and pinpoints children who are creative. Try to answer each question as truthfully as possible and, if you cannot choose an answer which specifically describes your child, choose one that is closest to the way your child usually behaves. There are no two questions or double meanings. A score of 118 and above is indicative of great creativity. A score of under 83 indicates that your child has lower than average giftedness. A score of 83 to a 117 indicates low average to high average giftedness.

Recognising
a gifted child

The gifted child will feel at home with situations and information that are unusual and ambiguous and which, on the surface, do not seem to fit together. He will enjoy all kinds of brain exercisers and teasers and may even find some of them very easy. A gifted child invariably learns quickly and is able to use that learning in a very broad sense. He exhibits extremely efficient and fast information processing, which is not only rapid but flexible too, and always makes good use of strategies and planning to use information.

While giftedness in itself is not a problem to the gifted child, it can become one because of the reaction of others. Some parents misunderstand their children, some children misunderstand their parents, and a gifted child, therefore, may become introspective. While this is not necessarily a cause for concern, if a gifted child becomes a loner and draws on his own imagination, he may become isolated at the time when he creates and manipulates ideas.

Some gifted children are so eager for information and learning that their enthusiasm is infectious but, even so, they need their parents to discuss with their teacher the kind of more specialised or accelerated learning they require, and to make certain they get it. And you may have to intervene in an assertive way on behalf of your child because despite what teachers may say you undoubtedly know your child's personality better than anyone who sees him for a few hours a day only, and only in a school situation.

Because giftedness includes exceptional specific talents such as musical or artistic ability, special mathematic or linguistic ability, or spatial ability, which might allow your child to play chess to a very high standard, in addition to a very high I.Q., your difficulty in finding sufficient stimulation for your gifted child is increased because we now see giftedness as more than a single entity.

There is no question that accelerated learning programmes do help; a gifted child may become bored and frustrated with classwork, which is too easy, and become troublesome in class simply because the usual lessons do not excite her. In this case, it may be necessary for your gifted child to fly over a form(s) to work on lessons with children who may be two years ahead in terms of age.

However, intellectual activity may so far outstrip personality development that you may become concerned about placing your gifted child in a higher graded school for example because of fears that the child will not be able to cope socially. But put your mind at ease; this has been contradicted by an amazing study of gifted children where fifteen hundred high I.Q. children from Californian schools in the 1920's have been followed throughout their lives to their sixties, seventies and eighties.

The investigators found that gifted children were better off than their less gifted peers in many ways besides performance in class. They were healthier, they were interested in many things such as hobbies and games, and they were more successful in later life. Both the boys and the girls in this study went on to complete many more years of education, than was typical of children of their time, and had more successful careers as adults.

There is some evidence that gifted children do come from family environments that enrich the child's experience of life, and there is some evidence to show that children born into middle-class families are more likely to receive that extra boost of stimulation, which turns bright into gifted. On the other hand, there is very little evidence to show that the parents of gifted children are "pushy" and force their children to study against their will.

HOW TO ENCOURAGE GIFTEDNESS IN YOUR CHILD

□ *Allow free time for play and do not interrupt your child all the time; observe more and intervene less*

□ *Provide areas of activity where things can be arranged that invite your child to become more involved*

□ *Provide simple toys that require your child's imagination to complete rather than complicated ones*

□ *Encourage your child to play outdoors so that she has contact with the world of nature and opportunities to play with sand, soil, water, and air*

□ *Give your child examples of real work so that he can imitate it; let him help you to clean up, wash the dishes, cook; these activities will become integrated into his play, and they help him to learn about life*

□ *Provide some artistic activities that allow your child to express her e.notions freely such as painting with fingers, a brush or a sponge, using bright attractive colours; this will not only help your child to express herself but also to learn about colours*

□ *Teach your child to record thoughts, discoveries, and questions on paper or audio/video tapes*

□ *Tell your child stories, particularly fairy stories, because they provide nourishing images that his imagination can build on*

□ *Limit the amount of time that your child spends watching television, video cassettes, and films (see p134)*

Parenting a gifted child

Being a good parent to a bright child is an enormously difficult job because the tendency is to become bogged down in the day-to-day task of raising children and therefore not keep the larger picture in perspective. Part of our task as parents is to see the spiritual in the mundane, to recognise the inner light in a child and the way, for instance, that a child's drawing might give you a picture of his emerging consciousness.

It is also our job to show a child, especially a bright one, the spiritual experiences in the everyday world so that, for instance, you can teach her to "see a world in a grain of sand – and an eternity in an hour" thereby transforming your child in the process.

Being the parent of a gifted child takes a tremendous amount of energy, too, and we have to be gentle to ourselves and patient with our own shortcomings. We have to practise kindness towards our own development as parents, and not be too self critical.

It is essential that you keep your own energy replenished otherwise you will become short tempered, impatient, and argumentative so you must make sure that you get adequate sleep particularly while your children are young. All of us, of course, want what is best for our children but most first-time parents know very little about being parents or how to bring up children. Very often you have to learn as you go, and that is uncomfortable. Nonetheless, such experiences provide many opportunities for growth for you as parents as well as for your children.

As your child's first teacher you absolutely must provide an atmosphere of love and warmth, calm and rhythm, interest and enthusiasm, all of which are vital to her growth. You are not expected to be an expert with your gifted child. You are simply expected to see a new way of being able to take account of all aspects of your child's

development be it physical, emotional, intellectual, or spiritual. You, therefore, help your child to meet the challenges of our changing world and get the best out of her life.

It is important for you to remember that your special child is not a little adult. He does not think, reason, feel, or experience the world as you do. Under the age of seven most children are centred on their bodies. They are growing very fast and they have the need for movement and physical exercise. Remember that your child learns primarily through example and imitation. In addition, repetition and rhythm through daily routine are vital elements in the healthy world of the young child, and provide security and confidence. Your child takes in information without blocking it out or filtering it, and for this reason, we have to pay attention to the quality of the environment in which he lives and the experiences that he enjoys.

There is a need for a balance between stimulation and protecting your child's senses. Stimulation from artificial sources such as television and films has quite a different impact on your child's mind from stimulation of your own voice, interests, and caring attention.

Understand that everything in your child's life is taken in so deeply that it can be transformed and come out again in creative play. Creative play is, therefore, food and drink to a gifted child, and it is essential to provide time and appropriate materials for this kind of play so that your child can work her way into everyday life by imitating through her play everything she experiences. Allowing the natural impulse of creative imagination to flourish is one of the greatest gifts that you can give your child.

Enrichment programmes

These give gifted children extra lessons outside of those in the normal school curriculum, so they might include for instance, a foreign language or a musical instrument. Enrichment lessons might also simply take the child deeper into a subject than other children studying the same course. So in ancient history, for example, the class might study the Trojan War, with the story of the Trojan horse, but the brighter children might be given extra lessons on the kind of life the Trojans led, their diet, their hobbies, their clothes, their art, their pottery, their jewellery, etc.

An important point about enrichment is that it must be qualitative enrichment. There has to be some kind of advance or expansion, it must not simply be more of the same.

Summer schools can provide another variety of enrichment programme but not as satisfactorily as an educational programme that continues throughout the year. However, if you do not have a programme for gifted education in your area you can give your child at least the chance of several weeks, enlarging her curriculum and acquainting her with other bright children. Research has shown, however, that a well-educated adult, in the environment of a promising child such as a parent, a relative or a friend of the family, who influences the child early can be very helpful, if they can find the time to lead, guide and teach in regular sessions, perhaps two or three evenings a week.

THE UNDER-ACHIEVING CHILD

The child who falls into the left-hand side of the curve on page 58 shows certain characteristics from birth, which some parents ignore because it makes their life easy, or because they do not want to face up to the fact that their child may be mentally below normal. If you ever find yourself saying any of the statements below, it should suggest to you the idea that your child needs testing.

"She is always a very good and quiet baby and hardly ever cries."
"We hardly know we have him; he never gives us any trouble."
"Sometimes she just lays in her pram without moving at all, and she sleeps a lot."
"He is as good as gold, a marvellous baby and no trouble, unlike his brother."
"She hardly makes a sound; she seems to live in a world of her own."
"He only just seemed to come alive when he was about eight months old, he never moved much when he was younger than that."
This kind of baby is nearly always late in developing everything (except perhaps sitting up and learning to walk); nearly always the first sign is a lateness in noticing things and in smiling. Occasionally, even blindness may be suspected because the child appears to take no notice whatsoever of what is going on around him.

Your baby even may be late in responding to sound, though when you come to do some tests for hearing (see p98), hearing is really quite normal. Sometimes your child may be late in learning to chew, which may lead to difficulty in eating solids or lumpy food.

Some of the milestones last longer than they should, for instance, the grasp reflex may persist beyond three months, or hand regard may go on for as long as 20 weeks (see p43). Similarly the taking of all objects to the mouth, mouthing, which is quite normal for children of six to twelve months, may go on for longer in retarded children.

The desire to throw things over the pram, casting, usually stops around 16 months but may go on longer if your child is mentally slow. A child of 18 months may be seen still slobbering if she is mentally backward where this should have stopped at around about a year. Lack of concentration and interest are all features of a mentally

interest may indicate impaired mental ability as may aimless over-activity. Pointless over-activity may not show up for a time, and children who were excessive sleepers when they were very young undergo a remarkable transformation and are now unable to concentrate. They flit from one activity to the other – even flitting physically around the room transiently interested in many tiny things, and this escalates into frenetic activity that is very difficult to live with. This is particularly true of the autistic child (see p166).

Help for you and your child

There is no question that an under-achieving child can be helped from a very early age by parental interest, attention, stimulation with songs, chatter, books, games and educational toys. A generally stimulating environment based on listening, discussion and questioning will help your child reach his optimum potential.

This is borne out by a meticulous study on infant intervention schemes carried out by Craig Ramey in North Carolina in the 1980s. Infants who entered the study were those from very poor families whose mothers had low I.Q.'s, and they were enrolled in special day-care programmes eight hours a day, five days a week. (This does not mean to say that your child has to have such intensive help and education, it simply shows the effect of an education programme.)

The children entered the programme from six to 12 weeks of age until they were five years old, when they began kindergarten in an ordinary school.

The programme was stimulating and emotionally warm, very much the kind of special family characteristics that help children to develop. At the same time, there was a control group from similar backgrounds that did not receive the specially enriched programmes but did receive nutritional supplements and medical treatment while being brought up at home.

The results were unequivocal. At all ages the enriched daycare improved I.Q. scores significantly over the control group, who were reared at home before attending school without an enrichment programme. Furthermore, the difference between children who had attended a pre-school enrichment programme remained significant after a further eighteen months of regular school.

These results do not mean that mental retardation can be cured simply by giving children heavy doses of especially stimulating education in infancy. What they show is that the intellectual power of children who begin life with few advantages can be increased if richer stimulation is provided. The importance of these findings it seems to me is that parents who have children with slightly less mental power than their peers only can help if they try to provide an enriching environment in their own homes from infancy onwards.

THE AUTISTIC CHILD

To observant parents the signs of autism will show up before the age of 30 months. Your baby probably shows no interest in being picked up and cuddled. He may be one those "good" babies who lies still, and seldom cries, and sleeps a great deal. There may be spells of screaming for no apparent reason. Classically, later on, there is a profound retardation in speaking – the emergence of a single word being delayed until the age of five or six; quite often with an incorrect diagnosis of deafness. Very often an autistic child shows no ability to relate to adults, or even other children, and prefers toys to people. There are stereotype mannerisms, aversion of the gaze and hardly any facial expression in any situation. Different children display different aspects of autism so it is quite a difficult syndrome to pin down, but here are some general points concerning autism.

Autism is a very difficult life-long mental handicap. It is not thought to be caused by emotional trauma, and it may occur with other disorders including mental retardation. It affects four times as many boys as girls. Parents with autistic children are not cold; they are as warm and as loving as anyone else. About four to five people in 10,000 will have classic autism, and about 15 to 20 in 10,000 will have autistic like conditions – all in need of support and understanding.

Autism is a problem of inhibited communication. Autistic children exhibit inappropriate behaviour for their age, for instance, having a temper tantrum like a three year old but at the age of ten. Autism does not just impair verbal communication but all aspects of communication, so autistic children cannot recognise or interpret facial expressions, gestures, or different tones of voice – all necessary in the day-to-day scheme of relating to other people.

Because of their inability to communicate, autistic children will feel isolated and cut off and may develop other secondary problems including indifference to other people, problems in learning, problems in adapting to the demands of everyday life, and a narrow repetitive form of behaviour.

Children with autism go through various phases. In the years between two and five the behaviour is very difficult to manage because of over activity. Then, between the ages of six and twelve, there can be some improvement in social skills and in behaviour, but in the teens and twenties early problems may reappear. As they grow up, children with autism do become more conscious of people and develop responsiveness to them, especially with families and friends.

Out of every 100 children with autism, 5 to 10 will become independent adults, 25 to 30 will make good progress but still need support and supervision, and the rest, unfortunately, will remain severely handicapped and dependent.

Help for you and your child

The diagnosis of autism in your child may be an agonizing trauma because in a way you will feel that you have lost your child, certainly you may have lost the child you thought you had.

However, with appropriate care and education, people with autism can be helped to live their lives with as much dignity and independence as possible. A main source of guidance, help, and support is the National Autistic Society. It produces a range of literature on autism and education, which will help you with the care of your autistic child; it organises conferences and day courses to keep you up with the latest theories of education; it puts you in touch with special counsellors, special schools, and other people in your area who can share your problems.

Your isolation will be ameliorated and life will not seem so hopeless if your child is integrated into a normal school by the age of twelve, which is a real possibility in about half the children.

Or, there are new special schools, where they believe in a philosophy of daily therapy involving group activities with an accent on music, drama and games and a reward system for progress and achievement, and a number of other therapies, programmes and treatments. Information about all of these can be obtained from The National Autistic Society.

"Holding therapy" is one of the techniques used with autistic children and it is worth enquiring about a group where holding is taught and practised. In holding therapy a parent forcibly holds her child despite crying, screaming, kicking, and struggling, and eventually the child quietens. This may take up to an hour, at which time the parent may be exhausted, but at the end of this time there is a rewarding phase of loving, affectionate, gentle, tender, touching between your child and yourself as the child learns to respond to you and to relate to you and is obviously giving and accepting love.

THE CHILD WHO STUTTERS

Many famous people have stammered including Moses, Aristotle, Virgil, Charles I, Lewis Carroll, Somerset Maugham, Charles Darwin. Stuttering usually starts between the ages of two and four and rarely begins after seven, and it is three times commoner in boys than girls – at least when they are young. The personality of your child is also important; the more sensitive a child is by nature, the more likely he is to stutter. More placid children or those who are even tempered are less likely to stutter.

The good news is that four out of five children lose their stutters spontaneously. A mild stutter is more likely to cure itself than a severe one, and in about three per 1000 of adults the stammer persists.

Most children when they are learning to speak go through a phase of stuttering or stumbling particularly when they are excited or upset, and they will nearly always lose this unless they are ridiculed or criticised for it or, more importantly, unless a parent becomes worried about it. Parents can precipitate their child into full stuttering by drawing attention to the stutter, telling their child to repeat himself, to speak clearly, or to take a big breath before he speaks. This makes him even more self conscious.

It is unquestionably unkind to your child to draw attention to stuttering. You should do nothing at any time by word, expression, or gesture, that calls attention to, or interrupts, your child's speech, because insecurity is a common factor in causing stuttering.

Help for you and your child

Treatment can be highly successful but all methods do have some failures so do not be disappointed. A favourite method is "timed syllabic speech" when your child is taught to pronounce all syllables with an equal space in between them each equally stressed. Another treatment is "shadowing" consisting of teaching your child to repeat syllables and words after they have been said.

It is known that stutterers can speak fluently if they do not hear their own voice coming back, and this can be done with "delayed auditory feedback" – a tape recording of your child's voice which she hears on earphones after a brief delay of a split second before transmission. This makes her speak very slowly indeed; she prolongs her speech sounds and the stuttering may stop.

Above all, seek the help of a speech therapist, which is available through your local health authority. You do not have to consult your doctor in order to get in touch with the speech therapy department.

In all cases of delayed or indistinct speech, hearing should be tested. Cases of persistent lisping should be enroled with the speech therapist for the appropriate treatment.

THE CHILD WITH A LEARNING DISORDER

Delayed speech development often occurs before learning and reading disorders, and there is some evidence that learning disabilities start in your two-year-old child. They very often occur along with poor coordination, repetitive movements, poor memory, and the inability to do formboards and drawing (see p110).

Delay in learning to read is usually part of a wider spectrum of learning disorders including difficulty in spelling, writing, and learning languages, for example. This compound disorder of language, often called dyslexia, may be defined as a reading age of two years or more below the mental age.

Delayed reading may simply be a normal variation, nearly always familial, but not necessarily in a mentally retarded child. However, a child who is mentally slow is more often retarded in learning to read than in any other part of school lessons. Common features that go along with retarded reading are a short attention span, aimless over-activity, defective concentration, impulsiveness, aggressiveness, and clumsiness. Your child's visual perception should also be tested.

A child should never be labelled dyslexic unless the diagnosis has been made with the help of expert, psychological advice. Nearly always there is a family history of the same complaint, or at least a learning disorder. Dyslexia is four times more common in boys and nearly always occurs in both of twins. Sometimes there are problems of laterality which means left or mixed handedness, and a tendency to read from right to left to reverse letters.

Dyslexia is made worse by many factors including the age of the parents, poverty and unemployment, lack of suitable reading ma-terial in infancy, lack of to and fro conversation, domestic friction, child abuse, sexual abuse, a one-parent family, or any cause of insecurity. School factors will include poor teaching, lack of motiva-tion, and school absences. Poor teaching or critical teaching may convince a child that he cannot read, and so he stops trying, then teachers are liable to label him as a poor reader and he becomes one, so his inability to read turns into a self-fulfilling prophecy.

Dyslexia must have something to do with Western society because it is ten times more common in the West than it is in the East, despite the fact that China has ten thousand letters in common use out of a total of about fifty thousand.

Help for you and your child

Many children grow out of their dyslexic difficulties without special help though some may have slight spelling difficulties for all of their lives. However, do seek special help. Your child's teacher at school or your local headmaster will put you in touch with a psychologist or a special teacher who is experienced in remedial teaching for dyslexic children. Your child may have to attend special classes in the evening several times a week for several years.

Your support and enthusiasm for your child's special lessons, progress, and achievements is irreplaceable; you must bear in mind that whatever type of remedial teaching is being used, your child cannot help it and is not just being naughty or stupid. Please tell your child that many famous and eminent people who have gone on to achieve much have experienced exactly the same problem as he. Auguste Rodin, one of the greatest sculptors of all time, was described as "the worst pupil in the school." His father said, "I have an idiot for a son" and his uncle said, "He is ineducable." Rodin never mastered spelling throughout the whole of his life but this did not prevent him excelling at his chosen profession.

The National Dyslexic Association will give you support, advice, and information about local schools and self-help groups, where your child's problem and your own difficulties will be treated sympathetically and patiently. It will also provide you with leaflets and books, which will help you to understand and care for your child.

THE HEARING IMPAIRED CHILD

Children must hear to speak, and they must speak to learn, read and write, so it is essential that you pick up any hearing impairment early in your child's life with appropriate testing (see p98) and undertake remedial action as outlined. You should always have your child's vision tested too, to make sure it's up to par.

Help for you and your child

Most children with hearing loss can function quite well when a hearing aid is fitted, and many physicians now fit them during infancy rather than waiting until pre-school age. The situation is somewhat different for the profoundly deaf, those children whose hearing loss is so severe that even with assistance their comprehension of sound and language is significantly impaired.

One basic point to remember is that if the emphasis is placed exclusively on oral language, the deaf child has much more difficulty in developing either speech or reading. If taught sign language, lip reading, and oral language at the same time, children find speech and reading much easier. Some children can progress fairly well in the normal school environment but even with good early training profoundly deaf children require special schooling. The aim should always be to educate your child to a standard where she can be integrated into learning alongside children with normal hearing.

THE SIGHT IMPAIRED CHILD

Blindness, if considered from the point of view of your child's ability to function in normal settings, including school, is a lesser handicap than deafness. This is because language plays an enormous part in learning, forming, and maintaining social relationships. Your blind child can learn to read with braille, and talk to others, can listen to a teacher, and can carry on conversations with you.

Nonetheless there are important limitations on blind children – the earliest being impairment of the relationship with you. Blind babies do not make eye contact as do sighted babies, so they do not look right at their parents and, through no fault of their own, parents may not respond to their blind baby the way they do to a sighted one. Attachment may be less, and a blind baby may feel less secure.

Even though a blind baby smiles at the same time as a sighted baby, a blind baby's smiles become less and less frequent while those of the sighted baby become more frequent. In addition, a blind baby's smile is much less intense and more fleeting.

Parents sometimes report feeling "rejected" by their blind baby. As a general rule, the facial expressions of a blind baby are sober and not expressive, and you may conclude that your blind baby is depressed or indifferent to you. It would be understandable if you withdrew gradually from your baby but it is very important that you do not; you must continue to talk, play, read, laugh, and give your blind baby just as much attention as a sighted one.

Fortunately, you can overcome any distancing that you may feel by learning to read your baby's other signals. While your blind child's face may be relatively expressionless, her hands and body move a great deal to express her feelings. So, for instance, if your child stops moving when you come into the room this means that she is listening very carefully for your footsteps. In the same way, she may start to move her hands rather than smile when she hears your voice. Your baby is trying to attach herself to you in different ways from a sighted child, and you have to learn to pick these up. Then, you can establish a close relationship. Once you start to read to your child you will provide more varied stimulation to which your child can respond.

What is critical for both you and your blind baby is early intervention, so that you, your family and your child get help and avoid potential emotional and intellectual problems. Seek help from your doctor early; ask for a referral to a special centre for blind children where you will find counsellors and psychologists who will show you how to best help your baby.

Help for you and your child

It is now possible to find out before your child is one year old if he has anything wrong with his eyes, and to have glasses fitted to correct his problem. A new test has been pioneered in Cambridge using a T.V. screen for assessment which can give you the results straight away, so there is less worry for you.

A series of video pictures is taken of your baby's eyes and the images are relayed onto a T.V. screen for assessment. The first image shows the baby's eyes in focus, two further pictures are then taken with the baby's face out of focus. If your baby is focusing on the camera her eyes will appear as bright dots, but if she is focusing behind the camera, for instance because she is long sighted, the images will appear blurred. This technique picks up babies whose eyeballs are also flattened and have astigmatism.

Parents whose children are borderline are asked to come back a few months later to see if the defect has corrected itself. Those who need correction are provided with glasses, and are given six-monthly check ups to see if their glasses need changing.

How you can help your child

Besides fitting glasses, there are certain things that you can do in the home to help your sight-impaired child. A child with poor vision needs stimulation by touch, noise, and smell, so choose toys that have interesting textures – rattles that make any sort of noise and any kind of smelly toy. Always point out the smells and textures of things to your child.

Colour is important to partially sighted children so choose brightly coloured toys in vivid yellows, blues, greens, and reds because they are easier to see than dull colours.

Only a partially sighted child can manage a jigsaw puzzle but puzzles are very important because they test thinking and spatial abilities. Choose ones with large, brightly coloured pieces that are easiest to see. Educational toys such as the formboards, finger puppets, and shape-sorters are just as appropriate for the partially sighted child as for the ordinary child.

All babies in their first year go through a stage of mouthing and exploring objects by putting them in their mouths. The child who is visually impaired is likely to continue this for longer than a sighted child, and so all toys should be easy to clean.

It is important that you choose a proper school for your partially-sighted child as soon as she reaches nursery age. An ordinary nursery is a good choice, if it is willing to admit your visually impaired pre-schooler, because it will provide your youngster with the normal range of pre-school activities, and give her the experience of mixing with other children of her own age. Do not worry if your partially sighted child at first seems timid; make certain the teacher knows your child's situation, so your child has careful supervision and encouragement, and usually the problem is quickly overcome. It helps, too, if there is a child psychologist with whom you can consult.

On the other hand, you may want your child to be under more expert care and you may want to enroll her in a specialist nursery set up specifically to meet the needs of the partially-sighted. The staff in these kinds of schools are usually specially trained, and particularly interested in the education of pre-school children with visual difficulties of different kinds.

The years up to pre-school for your child are very significant; you must be both stimulating and sensitive, and concentrate on your child's strengths and not on his visual weaknesses. This will guarantee that you give him a flying start.

THE PHYSICALLY DISABLED CHILD

The child with a handicap may need special treatment throughout his growing up but, most importantly, he needs to be treated naturally, and as much like other children as possible, particularly by his parents. Even with a serious defect, a child can grow up happy and outgoing, and should have the opportunity to learn to interact with other children from an early age.

It is important to come to terms with your child's condition so that you don't spend all your time wishing she was different, overprotecting her, or keeping her away from others. It is better not to dwell on any unhappiness or feelings of shame over your child's condition or appearance, particularly as pity will not help your child. Often, a parent will become so preoccupied with the handicap and its treatment, that he or she loses sight of their child as a person. Parents thus fail to enjoy all those good qualities that are unimpaired.

Many disabled children and their parents, therefore, can enjoy near normal family life. But, one of the most difficult problems a parent can face is to bring up a child with multiple handicaps or physical disabilities of such severity that the child cannot communicate, move or play. Some severely affected cerebral palsy children, for instance, cannot move without help, cannot speak understandably, and may be mentally retarded as well. It is very difficult but you must face up to the fact that your child therefore, will require full time care for the rest of her life.

How you can help your child

Remember your child can learn and love. The general feeling amongst health-care professionals, who look after severely or multi-handicapped children, is that intervention should begin very early.

Try to involve your family from the very beginning and by that I mean your whole family. This means you should be honest with any other children because they are going to have to make sacrifices; they will have to bear much of the brunt of having a severely handicapped brother or sister. The whole family has to learn not only how to care for and stimulate your handicapped child but possibly need help in developing their own love for the child. Brothers and sisters, in addition, need special attention so that they do not feel left out or sacrificed for the handicapped child. So each child is going to need their own special time with you.

Some children with chronic diseases such as cystic fibrosis or muscular dystrophy also have severe physical problems. It is important to get an early diagnosis and proper treatment because early intervention is critical. This is not just because your child's disease may be eliminated but because early intervention may prolong your child's life, its comfort, and enjoyment of life while life persists.

YOUR
CHILD
AND
SCHOOL

YOUR CHILD AND SCHOOL

We consider in Great Britain that a child is ready for school at the age of five, but, of course, this is not true of every child. Some children are ready for school a good deal earlier than five, and some up to a year later. If your child does not seem ready for school at five, this just means that he does not conform to an artificial standard age, not that he is backward. Most children thrive when they are in a class where they are not outstripped by the lessons, or the achievements of the children around them. There is nothing wrong in giving your child a growth year, so that he starts school somewhat later than his peers, because he will be much happier and do better at the top of a class than at the bottom. School can always wait; your child when ready will make up lost time in great leaps and bounds.

Play-based pre-school is an advantage for children from low socio-economic backgrounds (see p65) but for children from emotionally and financially stable homes, the advantages of pre-school are more difficult to pin down. Everyone accepts that the early years are enormously important times for teaching young children, but many experts think that your children learn best at their own pace at home. Formal education for children of four and under can lead to educational burn out and an early sense of failure.

If you go along to a good nursery school or kindergarten you will see that it is run along similar lines to a home with an interested and caring parent, but there are more children and it is more formal.

As a general guideline, I would suggest that if you and your child are doing well at home there is no need for you to seek out a pre-school educational programme. On the other hand, do not feel rejected if your child wishes to fly the coop and to start to play and learn with other children. You must follow the preferences of your child and your instincts. If your child is very bright, you may feel that she has outgrown the stimulation that the home can provide, and is really bored without company and more formal teaching.

CHOOSING A NURSERY

If you do feel that your child should be entered into kindergarten or pre-school, you have a heavy responsibility to investigate institutions, premises, and teachers, not to mention teaching style and the formality of each group. This will necessitate at least one visit to the nursery school as an observer and an interview with the head teacher and/or other teachers, so that you get a feeling for the atmosphere and the style. As you should go around a few schools before making a choice, use the checklist opposite for things to look for.

CHECKLIST FOR CHOOSING A SCHOOL

TEACHERS

☐ *How many teachers are there?*

☐ *Do the teachers appear to love children?*

☐ *What are the teachers' goals, aims and objectives for the children?*

☐ *What are the teachers' training backgrounds?*

☐ *What are the teachers' experiences in teaching?*

☐ *What are the teachers' experiences in mothering?*

☐ *Do any of the teachers have any children of their own?*

☐ *If so do they attend the school?*

☐ *Do you have rapport with the teachers?*

☐ *Would you feel happy leaving your child in the care of the school and its teachers?*

GENERAL ATMOSPHERE AND ENVIRONMENT

☐ *How many children are there?*

☐ *What is the environment like?*

☐ *Does the atmosphere feel calm or is it somewhat chaotic?*

☐ *Does the school feel safe?*

☐ *Is the heating efficient?*

☐ *Have attempts been made to make the school and its surroundings attractive?*

☐ *What is the curriculum like, is there a rhythm to it, providing a structure within which there is room for freedom as well as some more formal activities?*

☐ *Is there any indication that the children will get early reading instruction, desk work and work books?*

☐ *Do you get the feeling that imaginative play and toys are appreciated and encouraged?*

☐ *Do the children get the opportunity to play outside every day?*

☐ *What is the outdoor equipment like?*

☐ *Is there evidence of a television set (to be deprecated)?*

☐ *Are there simple computers available (best avoided with young children)?*

☐ *Is there evidence of artistic activities, like simple musical instruments, painting, sand-trays, water tables, dressing up box?*

☐ *How much music is there in the child's day?*

☐ *How long will the child listen to music on a tape or on a record?*

☐ *Are there singing and movement games?*

STARTING PRIMARY SCHOOL

It is unfair to send your child to school before she is ready. Starting school is a "hurrying" experience for a child (see p87), and it is quite easy for her to feel rejected if she does not enjoy the experience. Give your child the best possible chance of enjoying school by making sure that she is well prepared. There are certain basic skills that your child must acquire before she stands any chance of benefitting from her time at school, and it is worth making sure your child is reasonably well equipped with them before she begins classes.

Over the page is a checklist of the skills that you should have helped your child to acquire before she enters big school.

CHECKLIST OF SCHOOL READINESS

SOCIAL SKILLS

☐ *Is liked and accepted by other children and does not take up an aggressive or martyred stance when faced with difficulties*

☐ *Has the ability to share*

☐ *Is helpful about the house with chores, and is able to complete simple tasks*

☐ *Is quite comfortable when playing with a small group of friends*

☐ *Can look after her own personal needs like washing and drying her hands*

☐ *When a new activity is offered, is prepared to join in*

☐ *When instructions are given, is happy to follow them*

PHYSICAL SKILLS

☐ *Can deal with buttons, zips and shoe laces*

☐ *Can play finger games, is able to cut with scissors, can manage a large, blunt needle and thread, string beads, and other small skills of manual dexterity*

☐ *Can catch and throw a large ball, though not necessarily overarm*

☐ *Has sufficiently good balance to walk along a wall or a beam*

☐ *Can bunny hop*

☐ *Can hop a few steps on either foot*

☐ *Is not unduly restless or apathetic*

☐ *Is able to reach to her right shoulder with her left hand over the top of the head and vice versa*

MENTAL SKILLS

☐ *Can talk about a recent event or experience sensibly with some degree of fluency*

☐ *Enjoys stories and is able to listen without fidgeting too much*

☐ *Recognises colours and knows their names*

☐ *Knows her own last name, address, and telephone number*

☐ *Can remember, in essence, what her favourite stories are about*

☐ *Pronunciation, enunciation, making up sentences, is fairly fluent*

☐ *Already has memorised some childhood songs and rhymes*

☐ *Loves joining in singing whether tone-deaf or not*

☐ *Shows a desire to read and is interested in books or other reading material; comics are good enough*

☐ *In games that you play at home with other children, joins in and follows instructions when a new game is played*

Helping your child to like school

For most of her younger years your child has been home orientated and the majority of her interests are contained near or in the home. One of the ways of encouraging your child to take best advantage of all the learning experiences available at school is to increase her interest in school itself. There are certain simple ways of fostering a positive attitude to school.

Children who are brought up in homes where parents believe that childhood should be a totally carefree time of life usually develop a dislike of any activity that is similar to work. So these children like school as long as it is primarily play. But as soon as they move upwards through school and more and more effort is required to do the work they begin to dislike school. It follows, therefore, that having your child perform small tasks, giving him responsibilities, placing emphasis on imaginative and creative play, providing simple learning and memory tasks will help your child like school a great deal more and enable him to thrive there.

It is possible that attending nursery school and kindergarten makes adjusting to early school easier. What is certain is that children who are physically and intellectually ready for school have more favourable attitudes towards school than children who quite unready for their first classes.

Your own attitudes towards learning, education, and study will greatly influence your child's attitude towards school, different subjects, and teachers. A positive attitude is absolutely essential if you wish your child to enjoy school and get the most out of it.

It is very important for you to ascertain the emotional climate of the school and the influence of teacher attitudes and the type of discipline used. Teachers who have a good relationship with their pupils and use democratic discipline encourage pupils to like their schools. Teachers who are bored with their jobs, who have teacher's pets, who teach in a dull manner, and who are either too authoritarian or too permissive in their control of a classroom situation, have a negative effect.

Teacher-pupil relations are particularly important in how much your child likes school. A child who comes to school with a negative attitude towards teachers, which has been encouraged at home, is very unlikely to get on well, as her attitude towards all teachers tends to be unfavourable. The chances of your child liking school in this situation are limited.

Helping with schoolwork

All parents want to become involved in their child's school activities, and to help and encourage their child with schoolwork. To my mind it is a mistake to try to do this on your own simply by going along to a bookshop and buying learning books suitable for your child's age.

This could lead you to use methods that are different from those the child is using at school, resulting in confusion and a delay in your child latching on to lessons.

By far the best tack is to make an appointment to see your child's teacher with a view to discussing the sort of lessons your child is having, and the way they are taught.

If you really are interested in your child's progress you will make time to find out first hand what your child is learning, and the methods used in his particular school. Only in this way can you hope at home to reinforce the lessons your child is learning during the day.

Once you have formed a good relationship with your child's teacher, your offer of help in reinforcing school lessons at home will be welcome. You should ask the teacher in what way you best can help reinforce what is taught at school.

It may be that your child's teacher invites you to go along to the school to be an observer in some of the lessons. Some schools encourage parents to become involved in the actual teaching of children, especially in districts where the schools are rather short-staffed at times.

It is also true that many of the methods used by modern teachers are quite different from the methods that were used to teach us, and you may have to go through a whole new learning process to acquire the skills that your child finds so easy to master. This is the best of all possible situations because you and your child are learning together at the same time, having the same experiences, and together can share the joy of achievement.

So that your child remains familiar with the workbooks, equipment, and materials used in the school, you might ask his teacher if you can take some of them home on an overnight basis, so there is continuity in your child's education. This will make home learning easy for your child and limit the amount of frustration that you feel when there are lapses of understanding between you and your child.

Balancing your child's commitments at home and school

If you expect your child to suddenly accomodate his rapidly expanding universe, with the demands of school and home, you will be overstretching and "hurrying" your child.

Once your child has entered school your role becomes that of mediator, arbitrator, and balancer, helping him to reach some sort of comfortable equilibrium between school and home. If your child is going to get the most out of his school activities the home environment has to become less demanding and less arduous – in fact, a place of comfort and refuge. At the same time, however, a child can participate in home activities in different ways, which encourages his sense of responsibility, his sense of being a team member, and his sense of being trusted, and thereby makes him feel independent with status as an important individual in the family structure.

This is a time when positive social behaviour, helpfulness, accommodation, compassion, and thoughtfulness all can be recognised with very concrete rewards and privileges. These can be permissive rewards like treats, gifts, special outings and trips, but a far better way to reward your child is to discover what her interests are, and to take an active part in encouraging her to pursue them. Your reward can then be tailor-made to fit her hobby or special interest.

In addition, by becoming an enthusiastic participant in your child's interests you can be of real help in giving her the best chance of a healthy and happy life in the future.

From the age of five or six onwards children become interested in their bodies, their diet, their health, and their appearance. Almost every child, whether boy or girl, shows an interest in clothes – largely because they are the badges of belonging to a peer and/or gender group. If your child is interested in becoming a vegetarian, rewards and privileges can be to do with a healthy choice of diet. If your child is becoming interested in clothes, then you can satisfy some of his real needs by taking him to buy a new outfit and letting him choose the entire get-up.

UNDERSTANDING YOUR CHILD'S NEW WORLD

Besides giving your child status in the home you can increase her status outside the home by taking an interest in the symbols that mean a lot to all children.

Clothes and other status symbols

Clothes satisfy a child's needs to be an individual as few other things do. Babies express their need for independence by removing their clothes and trying to dress themselves. Pre-school children satisfy their needs by selecting the clothes they want to wear each day, and school age children form gangs and wear the clothes that are approved by the group.

Choosing his own clothes coincides with a child's idea of growing up; he begins to feel mature, and this is the time you can start to appeal to his sense of responsibility and thoughtfulness for others.

At a very early age, children discover that clothes have great attention value, particularly if they are brightly coloured, covered in badges, belts or ornaments, or brand new. Very soon after that they learn that their clothes identify them as individuals.

It is not long before your five year old learns that clothes also are symbols of belonging to a group, and satisfy a need which none of us grows out of. Around the same age, children become very concerned to demonstrate that they do not belong to the opposite sex and discover that clothes distinguish them from the opposite sex better than anything else. Clothes also help children who are self-conscious or shy, or who have physical defects, in that they can act as camouflage. By trial and error, a child can learn which clothes make the most favourable impression, aid social acceptance and, in the end, help improve self-image and produce a feeling of being happy with oneself and one's appearance.

Peer pressure and television shape ideas about other material possessions and status items, too, and your child may begin to have desires of which you don't approve. And while desires for these things should never be allowed to get out of perspective or pandered to, understanding them and keeping them in balance will help your child to find her way around a world where values are often distorted.

STATUS SYMBOLS COMMON TO MOST CHILDREN

☐ *Material possessions*

Toys and play equipment, sports equipment, clothes, collections of any kind including stamps, shells, some books, some comics

☐ *Family possessions*

A nice house with a playroom, a large lawn, a nice car or cars

☐ *Popularity with peers*

A large number of playmates and friends, especially those who are well liked by the peer group

☐ *Athletic success*

Success in games and sports at any age

☐ *Academic success*

Being a good reader, and among older children, good academic grades

☐ *Parental occupation*

Your occupation especially if it carries prestige or is professional can carry status for your child

☐ *Leadership roles*

A leadership role played by either the child or by the parents in business or community affairs is a status symbol for the whole family

☐ *Autonomy*

Having freedom to do what they want and when they want. Children who are brought up by overly liberal parents more often have this status symbol

☐ *Spending money*

Having a lot of money always impresses peers regardless of source

☐ *Earning money*

A child who earns money for odd jobs, gives the impression of being older than her peers and thus has the prestige status of being an earner

☐ *Travel*

The more children travel and the further away from home, especially by flying, the greater the status they seem to have with their peers

THE CHANGING RELATIONSHIP BETWEEN YOU AND YOUR CHILD

The basic change in the relationship between you and your older child is one of your giving up authority over him; you gradually let go of the reins, and your child takes over. You pass over the baton, run alongside to make sure your child is alright, and then drop further and further behind him as he takes off on his own.

You, therefore, will give up many of your roles, with varying degrees of pain and joy, and you will have to face up to relinquishing your responsibility, authority, rank, and protectiveness, and your roles as chief cook and bottle washer, money lender, time keeper, decision maker, and arbitrator who chooses friends and activities.

Helping your child towards independence

Gradually, you will have to relinquish your right to choose for your child in all areas of her life and allow her to exercise her own options while taking responsibility for her actions and their outcome.

By the age of six your child can take care of most of her personal and hygenic needs, and so can dress and undress herself, bath herself, and perhaps only needs help with washing her hair. She should be able to look after her school books, school bag, and sports kit. By the age of seven or eight, your child can even help with the laundry and other tasks that concern her needs. She also can take care of her room, and will want it a certain way.

By the age of eight, your child will want to choose her own clothes and many of her extra-curricular activities, and you should take her preferences into consideration. She also will be capable of being given pocket money, looking after it, and being given a very long rein in making decisions on how she spends it.

During all this time your authority will wane, and you should be pleased that you have a child who is capable of thinking for herself and expressing her independence, and you should not be trying constantly to hold her back. By the age of nine or ten, all children should have an equal voice in the family and have their comments listened to; their feelings, hopes, and desires always should be taken into consideration. They should be involved in any decision which concerns them, and it is just not allowed for you simply to pull rank.

I well remember the first time one of my sons, then 12, used logic to argue his case against mine. I was stunned and elated, and explained to him that every time he use logic to such telling effect he would almost certainly get what he wanted regardless of my wishes. This was the result of a long process that had begun when he was around four. At that time I started to encourage my son to show me how responsible he was, and to step by step negotiate freedoms, privileges, and permissions.

Avoiding over-protectiveness

Once your child has undertaken the enormous task of looking after himself at school it is simply unjust to be over-protective. Most parents have no idea how independent their children are, or what kind of difficult situations thay can manage on their own. Many six-year-old girls are looking after younger brothers and sisters, and seven-year-old boys are doing paper rounds. Over-protectiveness will simply stunt your child's desire for independence and his ability to be responsible. Claustrophobia in the home can ruin any chances of your child realising his own individual potential.

As your child gets older, of course, there is no need why you should be the only cook and cleaner in the house. He can be taught to cook simple meals, and boys very often love doing this. As your child matures, he even may want to provide meals for the rest of the family as one of my sons did, who later turned out to be an excellent cook. Your child also should participate in cleaning his own room, and certainly in keeping it tidy, though obsessiveness on your part about a clean and tidy room will only drive your child the other way.

Encouraging decision-making

As your child gains independence you can no longer be a clock watcher and time keeper; she has to be able to decide how long she wants to spend with her friends, or reading a book, or listening to music, within limits, but the more responsibility you give, the more responsible your child will be.

When it came to personal freedom I found that as I gradually gave my children more and more rope (with the proviso that they always had to let me know where they were by telephone, and state the time that they would return, and whether or not they needed me to pick them up), they gradually acted in a more and more responsible way, thereby earning more and more freedom because I could trust them. I told them so. Every time they kept to the agreement they were given a further privilege. This way they learned about the reciprocity of the contract between us.

Freedom and independence, of course, also extends to the friends they choose. You cannot decide your child's friends and she will only turn against you if you try to. It is not a good idea to express disapproval unless your child is really running wild with undesirable comrades, in which case you do have to put your foot down. However, in my experience, disapproving of a particular friend simply drives your own child in their direction and she becomes furtive. A far better idea is to tell your child to invite her friend home so that you can get to know him or her better. The friend may turn out to be a much nicer person than you think he or she is. Your child will sense your generosity and rise to your thoughtful gesture and be much more open to discussion and persuasion as a result.

USEFUL ADDRESSES

GENERAL

British Standards Institute
Linford Wood
Milton Keynes
Bucks, MK14 6LE
(0908) 221166

Child Growth Foundation
2 Mayfield Avenue
Chiswick
London, W4 1PW
(081) 9950257, (081) 994
7625

DISABILITY

Association for All Speech
Impaired Children (ATASIC)
347 Central Markets
Smithfield
London, EC1A 9NH
(071) 236 3632

Association for Brain
Damaged Children
Clifton House
3 St. Paul's Road
Coventry, CV6 5DE
(0203) 665450

Association of Child
Psychotherapists
Burgh House
New End Square
London, NW3 1LT
(071) 794 8881

Association for Research Into
Restricted Growth
7 Plover Rd.
Milbourne
Sherbourne, Dorset
(0272) 877243

Break Through (Deaf-
Hearing Integration)
Break Through Birmingham
Centre
Selly Oak Colleges
Bristol Road
Birmingham, B29 6LE
(021) 472 6447

British Dyslexia Association
98 London Road
Reading, RG1 5AU
(0734) 668271

Disabled Living Foundation
380–384 Harrow Road
London, W9 2HU
(071) 289 6111

Down's Syndrome
Association
153–155 Mitcham Rd
Tooting
London, SW17 9PG
(081) 682 4001

Invalid Children's Aid
Nationwide
Allen Graham House
198 City Road
London, EC1V 2PH
(071) 608 2462

Lady Hoare Trust for
Physically Disabled Children
(Association with Arthritis
Care)
37 Oakwood
Bepton Road
Midhurst
West Sussex, GU29 9QS
(0730) 813696

National Asthma Campaign
300 Upper Street
Islington
London N1 2XX
(071) 226 2260

National Autistic Society
276 Willesden Lane
London, NW2 5RB
(081) 451 1114

National Deaf Children's
Society
45 Hereford Road
London, WC1X 8PT
(071) 229 9272

National Library for the
Handicapped Child
20 Bedford Way
London, WC1H 0AL
(071) 255 1363

Royal National Institute for
the Blind (RNIB)
224 Great Portland Street
London, WC1N 6AA
(071) 388 1266

Royal National Institute for
the Deaf
105 Gower Street
London WC1
(071) 387 8033

Royal Society for Mentally
Handicapped Children and
Adults (MENCAP)
123 Golden Lane
London EC1Y 0RT
(071) 454 0454

Spastics Society
12 Park Crescent
London, W1N 4EQ
(071) 636 5020

EDUCATION

Advisory Centre for
Education (ACE)
18 Victoria Park Square
London, E2 9PB
(081) 980 4596

British Association for Early Childhood Education (BAECE)
111 City View House
463 Bethnal Green Road
London, E2 9QY
(071) 739 7594

MENSA (The High IQ Society)
Mensa House
St John's Square
Wolverhampton, WV2 4AH
(0902) 772771

National Association for Gifted Children
Nene College
Park Campus
Broughton Green Road
Northampton NN2 7AL
(0604)792300

FAMILY WELFARE

National Association for Maternal and Child Welfare
1 South Audley Street
London, N1 2XX
(071) 493 2601

National Child Protection Line
(0800) 181188

National Childminding Association
8 Masons Hill
Bromley
Kent, BR2 9EY
(081)464 6164

National Children's Bureau
8 Wakley Street
London, EC1V 7QE
(071) 278 9441

National Council for One-Parent Families
255 Kentish Town Road
London, NW5 2LX
(071) 267 1361

National Step Family Association
72 Willesden Lane
London, NW2 5RB
(081) 451 1114

SUPPORT GROUPS

Cry-sis (with Association for Parents of Sleepless Children)
B M Cry-sis
London, WC1N 3XX
(071) 404 5011

Hyperactive Children's Support Group
71 Whyke Lane
Chichester
West Sussex, PO19 2LD
(0903) 725182

In Touch (network for support groups)
10 Norman Road
Sale, Cheshire, M33 3DF
(061) 905 2440

TOYS

The Boots Company Plc.
Nottingham, NG2 3AA
(Children's World subsidiary company)
Alan House
Clumber Street
Nottingham, NG1 3ED
(0602) 411221

Early Learning Centre
Head Office
South Marston
Swindon, SN3 4TJ
(0793) 831300

Fisher Price Play Advisory Service Department
UFI Unit 14
Fairwood Industrial Park
Ashwood
Kent, TN23 2WY

James Galt and Co., Ltd.
Brookfield Road
Cheadle
Cheshire, SK8 2PN
(061) 428 8511

Mothercare
Head Office
Cherry Tree Road
Watford
Herts, WD2 5SH
(0923) 33577

Playgear Ltd.
3 Dennis Parade
Wunchmore Hill Road
Southgate
London, N14 6OA
(081) 882 1293

Tomy (U.K.) Ltd.
Wells House
231 High Street
Sutton
Surrey SM1 1LD

UNDER-FIVES

Pre-School Playgroups Association
61–63 Kings Cross Road
London WC1
(071) 833 0991

(VOLCUF) Voluntary Organisations Liasons Council for Under Fives
77 Holloway Road
London, N7 8JZ
(071)607 9573

INDEX

ACKNOWLEDGEMENTS

Child photography by Mike Good, Zartec Studios
Toy photography by David Murray

Typesetting by VAP, Kidlington Oxfordshire
Reproduced by Colourscan, Singapore

CARROLL & BROWN LIMITED
would like to thank the following:

Monica Orr for overseeing the toy chapter; Sara Cremer and
Elizabeth Thompson for their editorial assistance; Wendy Rogers
and Patricia Wright for modelling; Matthew Carroll for his
editorial assistance and for modelling; Howard Pemberton for his
computer expertise and assistance; Stephen Wright for supplying
the symbols; Jan at Zartec Studios for organising the models; and
the children at Chandos Children's Centre for their drawings.

The following companies very graciously lent the toys listed below:

Fisher-Price Toys. *Newborn to 6 months:* Dancing Animals Music Box Mobile; *7 to 12 months:* Chime Ball; *12 to 18 months:* Rock-A-Stack, Little Snoopy; *18 months to 2 years:* Chatter Telephone, Pull-A-Tune Xylophone, Tag-Along Turtle; Baby's First Blocks; *3½ to 5 years:* Play Family Marina, Casette Recorder with Microphone.

Tomy. *Newborn to 6 months:* Softlies Animals; *7 to 12 months:* Softlies Vehicles; *12 to 18 months:* Bring-Along-A-Song Record Player, Jazz Band Tambourine; *18 months to 2 years:* Bring-Along-a-Song Tape Player, Jazz Band Drum, Jazz Band Piano; *5 to 7 years:* Train Set.

The Boots Company PLC. *Newborn to 6 months:* Chirpy Pram Duck, Small Farm Animals, Aeroplane Rattle, Mouse Teether, Soft Animals, Roller Bell Rattle, Keys on a Ring Teether; *7 to 12 months:* Suction Rattle, Little Bears, Rag Books, Soft Cubes.

Early Learning Centre. *12 to 18 months:* Car Transporter, Stacking Bricks; *18 months to 2 years:* Zapf Baby Doll; *2 to 3½ years:* Doctor Outfit and Bag, Cleaning Set, Tool Kit, Picture Lotto, Duplo Plastic Bricks; *3½ to 5 years:* Magnetic Playset, Binoculars, Skittle Set; *5 to 7 years:* Minitill, Recorder.

Galt Toys. *7 to 12 months:* Boat Fleet; *12 to 18 months:* Wooden Transport Jigsaw; *2 to 3½ years:* Liquid Colours, Sticklebricks; *3½ to 5 years:* Magnifying Boxes, Duplo Plastic Bricks Truck; *5 to 7 years:* Construct-O-Straws, First Tapestry Kit, Picture Printing Kit, Catch-A-Mouse Game.

Nottingham Rehab Ltd. 0602-452345. Formboards 108, 109, 110.